THE
ADDICTIVE
ORGANIZATION

Anne Wilson Schaef
and Diane Fassel

1817

Harper & Row, Publishers, San Francisco

New York, Grand Rapids, Philadelphia, St. Louis
London, Singapore, Sydney, Tokyo, Toronto

The Twelve Steps reprinted with permission of Alcoholics Anonymous World Services, Inc. Excerpt from "The Productive, Integrative Organization" used by permission of Margaret Molinari.

FIRST HARPER & ROW PAPERBACK EDITION PUBLISHED IN 1990.

Library of Congress Cataloging-in-Publication Data
Schaef, Anne Wilson.
  The addictive organization.
  Bibliography: p.
  Includes index.
  1. Corporate culture—United States.   2. Organizational behavior.
3. Workaholics—United States.
I. Fassel, Diane. II. Title
HD58.7S29   1988   362.2'9   87–45720
ISBN 0–06–254841–7

ISBN 0–06–254874–3 (pbk)

90 91 92 93 94 MUR 10 9 8 7 6 5 4 3 2 1

This edition is printed on acid-free paper that meets the American National Standards Institute Z39.48 Standard.

DEDICATION

This book is for all of us who work with or relate to an organization and have wondered why we come away from our time at work or our meetings feeling crazy, off balance, and uneasy.

This book is for all of us who have moved into a new work situation with great hopes and expectations and found ourselves slowly ground down by the organization and losing our enthusiasm for the work we love.

This book is for all of us who feel we have to spend our whole weekend recovering from work only to go back and start it all again.

This book is for every troubled and/or hopeful organization that has spent thousands, even millions, of dollars on consulting packages and, even when the analysis has seemed accurate, has later discovered that there was no real or lasting change.

This book is for every organization that wants to understand why it continues to move from one crisis to another and is not able to focus on the kind of work it exists to accomplish.

This book is for every organization that truly believes that it is possible to make work-life healing and exciting and still maintain a good profit margin.

This book is for all consultants who genuinely want to be of service to the organizations with whom they consult and have not had the necessary conceptual tools to do what they want to do.

This book is for all of us who have intuitively known that there is something wrong with the way our organizations are structured and functioning and have been searching for the "missing pieces."

This book is dedicated to all those persons and organizations with whom we have worked, with whom we are working, or with whom we will work. May it provide a "missing piece."

Contents

Acknowledgments

We are grateful to numerous people for their encouragement during the development of this book. Our families and our community in Boulder offered their usual good humor and support. Gwen DeCino, Carol Ewer, John Reed, and Beth Wilson provided an environment that removed all obstacles to working on the book. Client organizations willingly became case material, following the development of our ideas with keen interest. Trainees and former trainees commented on the manuscript in seminars and several read it and made valuable input. Jan Johnson, our editor at Harper & Row, believed in the book from the first day she heard about it and she ably guided it through all phases of production. Finally, we acknowledge the influence of our fathers, Robert Fassel and Virgil Willey, two men who worked in the mainstream of corporate life yet taught us to see another way. To them and to all who have cheered us on in this effort, we are sincerely grateful.

All of the cases and examples we refer to actually occurred and are accurate. However we have changed the names, locations, and identifying details.

Introduction: A Missing Piece

Everyone in this society lives and works in some kind of organization, group, or system. Beginning with the family, moving into the school, the workplace, clubs, and civic organizations, most of us spend the majority of our lives within organizations or relating to organizations. In fact, in this society the person who cannot function organizationally is handicapped. We need to understand every aspect of organizational life. Moreover, a broadly focused book on organizations is needed, a book that will be read by corporate executives, entrepreneurs, and the members of volunteer groups and social and professional clubs alike. We saw the need for a book that will "name" our experience in organizations at all levels.

Even though there is a plethora of books about organizations and corporate life and millions of dollars each year are spent on consultants and packages designed to "fix up" what is wrong with organizations, corporations continue to search desperately for models that will reverse a slipping economy and enliven a poorly producing work force. Individuals look forward to weekends so that they can recover from their "crazy-making" experiences at work only to find that they must face the same dynamics on Monday. Often, persons who come from dysfunctional families find their organizations repeating the same patterns they learned in their families. Even though these patterns feel familiar, they do not feel healthy. Though consulting packages seem to alleviate some problems for a few days or a week, those same problems reemerge with even greater force and tenacity. Even after our favorite committees have had workshops on communication skills, breakdowns in communication, dishonesty, isolation, anger, and withdrawals continue. What is going on? What are we missing? As a friend of ours at a Fortune 500 company states in an internal memo, we are confused about something, and it is not clear what it is. In an in-house memo she wrote:

> What is a productive organization? We have been inundated in the last few years with books, articles, case studies, and news stories that describe the attributes of excellence and successful organizations. As a country of business people we have studied our competitors. At various times with various voices we have touted high tech, robotic, and electronic solutions. From Europe we have accepted a need for cooperation and collaboration with our employees by starting quality-of-work-life and employee-involvement efforts in major companies like GM, AT&T, and Ford. Unions like the UAW, the Communications Workers of America, and the Steel Workers became leaders in the changes. Yet many of these very hopeful programs have lost their initial charge. We have looked to the East and started Quality Circle, Just in Time delivery programs, Total Quality Control, Statistical Process Control, and Company-Wide Quality Control.
>
> Yet, through all of our writing and research, we still seem to be missing something. We are attracted to these demonstrations of excellence; we recognize that there is something that we do not have, yet the majority of executives and managers in the United States are unable to implement significant permanent change incorporating these ideas. What is it that we are attracted to? What is it that eludes us when we try to implement these changes?[1]

"What is it that eludes us when we try to implement these changes?" It is the response to this question that has impelled us to write this book about organizations. We believe that it is time to move to a new level of understanding about the organizations in which we live and work. Prior analyses have elements of truth in them, and at the same time a very important element has been systematically ignored.

Ironically, the very correctness of the analysis (even if partial) has been a factor misleading us to accept incorrect solutions. When the analysis has elements of truth in it and "rings true" for those involved, it is difficult not to become gullible and accept wholeheartedly the solutions offered. Unfortunately, this very gullibility may well be perpetuating the problem. For example, in Steven Prokesch's article in the business section of the *New York Times*, "Remaking the American CEO," we read that "many are adopting a new creed that puts corporate survival above all else. The result: a generation of ruthless management." As Prokesch describes it, "The new order eschews loyalty to workers, products, corporate structure, business, factories, communities, even the nation. *All such allegiances are viewed as expendable under the new rules. With survival at stake, only market leadership, strong profits and a high stock price can be allowed to matter*" (italics ours). Prokesch sees corporate leaders going through a massive rethinking process, and their response to the imperative to change has been to become more ruthless, more manipulative, more dishonest, more rigid, less creative, and less willing to take risks. We believe this response is indicative of what we have been missing in our understanding of organizations.

Through our work and research with groups and organizations, we have come to see the piece that has been systematically ignored: many of our organizations are addictive organizations embedded in an addictive society. By this we mean that many organizations are affected by addictions and an addictive worldview and even themselves function exactly like an active individual addict.

In *When Society Becomes an Addict,* Anne Wilson Schaef has demonstrated that addictive behavior is now the norm in the society, and that society itself functions as an active addict.[2] This is also true at the organizational level. Thus we have found an important missing piece, a piece of information that has been systematically overlooked in accepted analyses of the problem with organizations, and though an understanding of this "piece" may not lead us to all the needed solutions, it will dramatically shift the way we look at organizations and what we do with and in them.

We have begun to recognize that many of the behaviors considered "normal" for individuals in organizations are actually a repertoire of behaviors of an active addict or a non-recovering co-dependent. For example, the solutions quoted in the aforementioned article by Prokesch (ruthlessness, rigidity, dishonesty) are exactly the ways that an active drunk would respond to crisis. In addition, many of the organizational processes deemed "acceptable" in companies are just more of the same addictive behavior masquerading as corporate structure and function.

Why have those who work with and study organizations been so reluctant to recognize this reality? One of the reasons, perhaps, is that the basic defense mechanism of addictions is denial. In the treatment of individuals with addictions, the first step toward recovery is to break the denial system and admit having the disease. We know that historically social analysts and persons in mental health and the helping professions have generally been woefully ignorant about addictions. They have frequently functioned to patch up the problem, thus enabling the individual to limp along without ever confronting the real issue, addiction. Another powerful element is that persons coming from addictive families tend to think the addictive process is normal. Since it is the only process they have known for most of their lives it is therefore, for them, reality.

These two tendencies—to deny the presence of the effect of addictions and to see addictive behavior and processes as normal—have also been true in the field of organizational development and in the process of organizational consultation. As mentioned earlier, one of the reasons that many organizational and management techniques have not made lasting changes is that they have not really addressed the underlying problem. Though we ourselves admire a large part of the writing and work going on in organizational development circles today, our experience is that most of these approaches will not be fully effective until they recognize that many of our organizations are functioning addictively, both in terms of individual personnel and as a whole system. Unfortunately, the problem is exacerbated by the general lack of information about addiction on the part of internal and external consultants as well as EAP (employee assistance program) counselors.

Our experience is that addictive individuals and systems can and do begin processes of recovery that, though lifelong, do result in solid health and better, more productive functioning. This book will add another major, heretofore missing dimension to the understanding of organizations.

In this book, we explore the concept of the addictive organization—what it looks like, how to recognize it, how it functions, the processes and structures it sets up that keep it in its disease, and how it can begin the recovery process.

Section I explores the discovery processes we used to arrive at a working knowledge of the addictive organization, beginning with some of the organizational concepts that have been helpful to us. It is important to recognize ideas current today in organizational literature: excellence, innovation, Z-theory, quality circles, and organizational transformation. We then explore some of the important contributions to the field and also point out some ideas that are conspicuously absent. These are some ideas that are emerging outside traditional organizational development, management, and consultation that have been important to us, have contributed to our thinking, and have expanded our understanding of organizations. We demonstrate how they are relevant to organizational theory, development, and transformation.

It is here that we ask, What is missing in the previous conceptualizations? As we have said, the missing piece is an understanding of the role, power, and pervasiveness of the addictive process.

Section II is devoted to definition of terms: addictions in general, the characteristics and processes of addictions, the addictive process itself, co-dependence, and adult children of alcoholics. Even though there has been an explosion of popular information about addiction, we believe that there will continue to be general ignorance about addictions because learning about addictions must be a participatory process. By this we mean that getting logical and rational information about addictions is not enough. In order to truly learn about addictions, one must face up to one's own addictive patterns and begin recovery. Since the addictive process is the norm for the society, one must assume that everyone participates addictively at some level. This information-giving section is necessary to provide a common language and a common conceptual framework. This section examines what we mean by the addictive system, the addictive process, co-dependence, and adult children of alcoholics.

Section III delineates four levels where addiction impacts the organization and gives examples of these levels. Essentially, this section describes how the organization is an addict. We have been fascinated by the richness of this concept, and it is here that we explore four facets of the organization as addict.

The first aspect explored is the problem created when a manager or key person is an active addict. Examples are given of the effect this can have on an organization, and we examine some of the organizational ramifications of not confronting this problem. Persons in key positions have a powerful effect on corporations. Using selected examples, we show how much impact dysfunctional managers have on the whole system and on the employees with whom they relate.

A second aspect of the organization as addict is that scores of nonrecovering addictive and co-dependent employees are inevitably replicating their dysfunctional family system in the workplace. Family systems theory has long recognized that problems not solved at one level always occur elsewhere; this is also true of addicts and co-dependents in corporations. They do what they know best, and that is to operate addictively wherever they are.

A third part of our inquiry takes us into our theory that organizations themselves can and do function as the addictive substance. This process happens throughout the organization—in its mission, its products, its centrality as an organization in employees' lives, and in the loyalty it expects. This is especially seen in the high-performing companies. Then, we move into a pervasive, not well understood, basically ignored addiction: workaholism. Looking at workaholism is one way of viewing the evidence of the addictive process in organizations. It is important to see the role major institutions in this society have played in denying the meaning and reality of workaholism and in actually promoting it as socially acceptable, all because it *appears* to be socially productive.

The fourth aspect we probe is how an organization itself functions as an active addict. By this we mean that the organization exhibits processes and behaviors that are common to individual addicts. These behaviors are examined in detail, as are the overall structure of organizations as the context for addictive processes and behaviors. We explore how the structure and function of addictive organizations tend to perpetuate and patch up problems instead of facing and solving them. We also develop a description of the characteristics of addiction in organizations as evidenced in communication, gossip, fear, isolation, dishonesty, suppressed feelings, sabotage, projection, disrespect, confusion, control, denial, forgetfulness, self-centeredness, dualism, grandiosity, and planning as a form of control. We explore these characteristics using examples and cases from a wide range of service, technological, and industrial corporations as well as nonprofit organizations.

Paradoxically, all four of these facets of the organization as addict are distinct elements, yet they are also interrelated aspects of the organization. They can exist separately, yet they frequently support one another, and hence they are usually found interrelated and intertwined.

Section IV deals with the process of recovery in the addictive organization. Obviously the addictive organization cannot be approached with the usual, traditional tools of the change agent or consultant. This chapter highlights specific aspects of recovery for an addictive organization.

The role of the consultant in relation to an addictive organization differs from what that role has been traditionally. We clarify that difference and give attention to problems of traditional consulting practices. We look at instances in which consultants can and do become enmeshed in the addictive system and reconsider the issue of objectivity. This section focuses upon the role of the consultant in a recovering organization and describes some potential new roles for consultants.

Section V explores the implications of the material introduced in the rest of the book. It describes the characteristics of organizations that are moving out of the addictive system. We include here a number of characteristics that are not new to high-performing organizations; the centrality of these characteristics *is* new, however. These include the mission being supported by structure, self-responsibility, permeable boundaries, multivaried-multidirectional communication, integrated work teams and situational leadership, a sense of morality in the way of working and in product development, congruence in formal and informal goals, and a commitment to a process model of change.

We conclude by posing questions our research and experience suggest. What does all this mean for the way we structure an organization and our society? Are there other questions? We believe that we have discovered some new and exciting options for organizations, which we explore in this section.

We have spent many years consulting with organizations. Our clients, whose experiences are reflected in this book, are multinational corporations, Fortune 500 companies, health care systems, agencies, churches, schools, religious orders, and family businesses. It has taken long hours of observation and dialogue with clients and co-workers to evolve and synthesize our thinking to the point where we have perceived this important "missing piece" about addictions. This information has been extremely helpful and effective in the organizations with whom we consult, and this book will offer valid and necessary tools for understanding organizations. As Prokesch says, quoting an Eastern Airlines vice-president, this corporate rethinking "is a process that can never stop. The ability to adapt to a constantly changing world is not only a requisite for success, but for survival."

The ideas about the addictive system and its evidence in organizations builds from section to section. We do not pretend that this book provides a quick fix for the problems troubling American organizations today. We recognize the magnitude of those problems. What we do propose, however, is that many of the superb proposals for turning around American business are essentially useless if they are being tried in organizations that share some or all of the characteristics of the addictive organization and do not include this "missing piece." In this sense, then, it is in the best interests of participants, employees, managers, and consultants to understand more about the addictive process that is rampant in the society, begin the process of recovery, and get on with the important mission of the organization in the marketplace and in the world today.

I

THE ORIGINS OF AN IDEA

The Origins of an Idea

We believe that we have developed a unique description of a process in group and organizational life. There were four strands in the evolution of these ideas that were important to us: organizational development, paradigm shift concepts, women's literature, and addictions research and treatment. There are many other areas that could have been probed and that have influenced us, but the ideas from these four consistently emerge in our work with groups. It is not only the importance of each of these areas, it is also the uniqueness of the combination that added to our growing awareness of the importance of addiction in organizations. The "uniqueness" does not exist in any one of these four areas per se, it exists in the combination. For example, we have found that few people knowledgeable about organizational literature are also well read in feminist, new paradigm, and/or addiction literature, and few in the addictions field have also digested writings by women or the literature on organizations, about the new paradigm, and so forth. This combination of ideas applied to organizations appears to be unique.

The idea of the addictive organization has been germinating in us for a number of years. As we said, it developed out of several concurrent forces in our lives. It came into focus, however, when we began looking at the role that addictions play in our personal lives, in our families, and in the lives of our friends. It was not long before we recognized that many of the groups we knew and the organizations with whom we consulted also have characteristics that we recognized as addictive. Observing some of the forces in our lives, we could link these forces to key concepts in contemporary writing that had been very important to us. This exploration slowly contributed to a full-fledged theory of the addictive organization. No new ideas develop in a vacuum. New ideas emerge from our thinking, our growing, our experience, and our surprises. As most of us know, creative ideas and awareness are not really developed, they are discovered. New ideas always somehow relate to new understandings of old perceptions or new slants on familiar material. Frequently, we discover what we have not yet known by moving slightly to the left or the right (or even standing on our head) and viewing the old from a new angle. However, in order to achieve that new angle, multiple strands have to come together to form a new perception. This is what happened to us in the development of the ideas in this book. We want to share how the idea of the addictive organization developed for us by exploring the major areas of scholarship and experience leading to our discovery of what we consider to be a major missing piece in understanding organizations and organizational change. We describe some key concepts in each of these four areas and show how they eventually built to another perception—that of the addictive organization.

ORGANIZATIONAL DEVELOPMENT

When we survey the literature on organizations written in the past three years and balance these writings with our training and experience, a few books and themes stand out as significant.

PARTICIPATION

One dominant theme pervading the field is participation. William Ouchi, in his *Theory Z,* summarizes the meaning and impact of the Japanese approach to participative management.[1] One of the key concepts, of course, is the quality circle. Almost everyone has heard of quality circles, and increasing numbers of American workers have participated in them. They are built on the belief that involved workers are essential to increased productivity. The quality circle is the vehicle for this involvement, as teams of workers sit down together to discuss problems in their area and to develop solutions to suggest to management. At times, workers are even free to implement changes.

A quality circle is a process that engenders active participation, encourages team spirit, distributes responsibility to the workers, and produces a high level of cooperation and "ownership" of the product. Quality circles have been the cornerstone of Japanese worker involvement and have been tried in the United States with varying degrees of success.

Why has such a concept taken hold in the capitalist countries? Certainly corporations are concerned with falling productivity and the need to become more competitive in the world market. In addition, we believe that worker participation is indicative of an overall change in organizations from the highly industrialized model to a technological "flattened" hierarchy style.

We have found Ouchi's ideas and those of others on worker participation very useful, because the heart of the theory is based upon the belief that people must take responsibility for their own lives, experience the consequences of their actions, and learn from them. When employees are removed from giving input, they cannot deal with the consequences of their actions, and they are, therefore, less able to assume personal responsibility. Also, it is important to recognize that full personal participation results in a totally different kind of knowledge and information from that which is gathered abstractly and objectively by someone else. This kind of information in turn affects the organization differently from the information of nonparticipatory management. Quality circles make available a wider pool of talent and foster a climate in which people learn from one another. We have seen numerous groups spurred on by a few words of affirmation or by the sheer excitement of solving a problem, which suggests that money is not the only incentive important to workers.

We think quality circles and other forms of worker participation result in less segmentalism and more communication between groups in organizations. Such participation also distributes leadership among more people, in turn allowing them to learn the skills of leadership. This "spreading around the wealth" challenges the notion that leadership resides in just one appointed person. It is general knowledge in organization circles that with worker participation there appears to be less sabotage of products and fewer sick days taken, suggesting participation is healthy for both worker and company.

Marshall Sashkin's article "Participative Management Remains an Ethical Imperative" is characteristic of much of the writing about this topic in that it provides a summary of the forms of participation.[2] However, his article is considered controversial because he insists that participation is a moral obligation. Briefly, he sees four possible areas of participation by workers: setting goals, making decisions, solving problems, and planning and carrying out change. These four can be done by the individual alone, employee-management pairs, or a group or team. Sashkin concludes that highly nonparticipatory jobs cause psychological damage and long-term physical harm, whereas participative management, when properly designed and implemented, improves performance and physical and psychological health. Thus, participative management is an ethical imperative if one holds that it is wrong to do physical and psychological harm to others.

Historically, the heightened emphasis on worker participation is a continuum of the debureaucratization of the workplace. Workers are now seen as persons, not objects to be used. They are no longer cogs in the wheel of manufacturing or the nonentities of a large service agency. The concept of worker participation has been widely accepted and now pervades every aspect of our world, from Nicaraguan peasants living in village groups to high-powered think tanks in corporations.

Having come of age in the era of participative management, and having belonged to myriad work groups, T-groups, and self-help groups, we came easily to the notion of worker participation in our consulting practice. What we have found, however, is that in practice, participative management is frequently a rhetoric of management that protects the seat of control and power at the top. Interestingly enough, we have found those groups, like the church, that are supposedly "more moral" are also frequently very deceptive about participative management. For example, there may be a stated belief that the poor need to participate in decisions that affect them, but operationally they are not included in financial planning because they "do not have the skills." As in feminist groups, we have also seen the need to have no leaders become itself a tyranny. Such experiences with groups who claimed a commitment to full participation yet reneged in subtle and significant ways led us to question whether management views everything, even participation, as a means to satisfy its need for control. We began to appreciate Ouchi's and Sashkin's insistence that the key to successful participative management is training for it and effective methods of implementation. We could see that key issues were being raised by participatory management, yet something seemed to be missing with respect to the context in which these issues were raised.

A further question emerged from our experiences with participative management. We began to wonder about the relationship between objectivity and participation. Berman has said that the scientific era has been one of objectivity, in which we have become observers of ourselves rather than active participants in our own experience.[3] Was participatory management a reaction against this century-old belief, and was a switch to full participation part of our larger system shift? The answers seemed to elude us, and we determined to keep this question in the forefront as we continued to explore the function of organizations.

Finally, Sashkin's insistence that participatory management is an ethical imperative challenged us to move beyond the usual criteria: Is this change efficient? Is it effective? We begin to ask, Is this change right? Is it life-enhancing for the individual, the organization, and the society? We soon became aware that if changes are not life-enhancing on all these levels, they are not life-enhancing at all. Such queries opened new avenues to us and the groups with whom we work.

Innovation, Change, and Transition

A second major theme pervading organizational life is innovation, change, and transition. Innovation is defined as something more abrupt than an incremental change; incremental changes involve minimal disruptions, whereas innovation requires major adjustments in structures and functioning. Innovation is the (usually messy) process by which new, creative ideas are fostered, developed, and implemented. Innovation is a response to the constant change in the marketplace that puts pressure on the corporation to create products and adapt products in order to acquire a larger share of the market. In the public sector, innovation is related to staying close to the consumer so that services are relevant to their needs.

Two early books that deal with innovation as a process are Everett Rogers, *Diffusion of Innovation*, and Gerald Zaltman, and others, *Innovations in Organizations*.[4] The first describes innovation as phased change occurring over time. The second deals with the effect of the structure of management on the change process.

A more recent book by Rosabeth Moss Kanter, *The Change Masters*, describes the kind of context that fosters innovation.[5] Kanter observes that 1960–1980 has been a "transforming era"—a time when societal circumstances have changed sufficiently to warrant a major shift of assumptions within the organization. She contrasts the traditional characteristics of the industrial corporation of the 1890s to the 1920s with the emerging characteristics of the 1960s and 1980s.

Kanter's main response to the new environmental challenge is to propose some keys to innovation. She thinks it is imperative to see problems as wholes related to larger wholes. One of her main proposals is to call for integrative action in place of segmentalism. She sees segmentalism as a tendency to wall off and compartmentalize actions, events, and problems, thus keeping each piece isolated from the others. This process leads to a high level of overspecialization and to limited exchanges among the segments. Kanter feels segmentalism inhibits innovation and limits the motivation to see and solve problems. She believes that as groups isolate, they tend to take on problems that are particular to their areas and that this limits their ability to respond to and focus on problems that are not "theirs." Furthermore, when people's activities are confined solely within their job description, it is less likely they will ever dream or go beyond set parameters.

This segmentalist style effectively quashes the entrepreneurial spirit and sets up secretiveness and competition. It is used when a high degree of certainty is valued and the focus is to keep the organization on a steady course. This style also serves to keep at bay the new and the unprecedented. (Interestingly, it perhaps produces more upheaval than does gradual change.)

Kanter develops a scheme by which she thinks the spirit of innovation can be engendered in corporations. We think one of her suggestions is very relevant to our work with organizations. She says that a

> requirement for empowering people to reach for a future different from the past is respect for the individuals in the organization. For people to trust one another in areas of uncertainty where outcomes are not yet known, they need to respect the competence of others. In segmentalist companies, the system is trusted more than the individual. Indeed the system is often designed to protect *against* individual actions.[6]

Behind Kanter's work is an important historical shift that relates to how culture views change. We know that change appears to be accelerating at a tremendous rate, and concomitantly our view of change is also changing. In the past, in the dominant system of the culture, change was not considered "normal." It was an upheaval or crisis that forced one to do something different. This was followed by a period of stability, shattered by another change; however, there was pressure to get things back to stasis and therefore, security. Kanter and others writing in this area take the position that change is a constant, only the rate of change and kind of change varies, or as C. S. Lewis says in *Perelandra*, even "the mode of change itself is changed."[7]

Given our understanding of the work of Kanter and others on innovation and the response of organizations to change, we have pondered the behaviors we have observed in organizations relative to change. First of all, we see again that the rhetoric is different from the behavior. Though there is a stated belief that change and innovation are possible and even desirable, there is often a single-minded dedication to stasis. The idea of planned change is still rare (and even "planned" change is based on the illusion of control). The expectation is that crisis often precipitates change and change can only take place following a crisis. This leads to a crisis orientation and the illusion that confusion is the normal by-product of innovation.

Segmentalism exists when individuals isolate from other workers and other groups. Segmentalism impedes innovation. This kind of isolation produces a kind of tunnel vision that creates power blocks within the organization, all of which ultimately become a subversive form of control. In addition, segmentalism contributes to the creation of rigid boundaries. Rigid boundaries, as we have seen them, become impenetrable to information coming from the outside environment, from co-workers, and even from inside oneself. The function of these rigid boundaries appears to be to control or eliminate paradox and ambiguity as well as the sometimes messy ideas that lead to innovation.

No consideration of innovation would be complete without a look at the excellent company research exemplified by Peters and Waterman's *In Search of Excellence* and Peters and Austin's *A Passion for Excellence,* both popular books on the "how" of innovation.[8]

In Search of Excellence develops eight basic principles for staying on top of the heap. In abbreviated form they are (1) a bias for action, a preference for doing something, anything, (2) staying close to the customer, (3) autonomy and entrepreneurship, (4) productivity through people, (5) a hands-on value-driven executive style, or keeping in touch with the essential business of the firm, (6) sticking to the knitting (i.e., remaining with the business the company knows best), (7) a simple form, lean staff, and (8) a simultaneous loose-tight property, which means a dedication to the values of the company, the form of implementation being not so important.

A Passion for Excellence distills these eight down to four: customers, innovation, people, leadership.

There have been many rave reviews of the excellent-company material. Perhaps its significance is in methodology as well as results. These are two books that move away from negative thinking about companies. Instead of focusing on what is wrong, the authors look at what is right. In the process the authors were taught by the companies they researched, and they proceed from their practical experience to the formulation of abstract principles. Peters, Waterman, and Austin are not the only ones who observed excellent companies for solutions to organizational problems. Kanter used a similar method, although her conclusions tend to be more academic than practical.

The excellent-company material is simple, practical, and focuses on people. It is also reality focused. One of Peters and Waterman's suggestions opened an intriguing door for us. We had been considering their eighth principle, simultaneous loose-tight properties, which translates roughly: Be rigid about purpose, and allow chaos around implementation. It occurred to us that traditional bureaucracies have been characterized by red tape, rules, and rigid adherence to procedures, often causing them to lose sight of their essential purpose for being. The excellent companies insist on rigid adherence to purpose and allow high tolerance for chaos around procedures. This appeared to be a kind of dualism characteristic of the confused thinking we had met in companies in trouble. They fluctuated back and forth between the bureaucratic model and the excellent company model, believing that one or the other style was the antidote to the problem. This setting up of "one" or the "other" is dualism. When companies set up this kind of dualism they ultimately stay stuck, not seeing other options. We believe that dualistic thinking is itself the problem—*regardless* of the content of the thinking—and that confronting it leads to healthier functioning.

There is one aspect to the excellent company material that leaves us feeling uncomfortable: it is the single-minded, passionate dedication to the quest for excellence as defined in these books. Both books are highly motivational. They are also exhausting, even to read. Listen to Peters and Austin on the "cost" of excellence:

Even a pocket of excellence can fill your life like a wall-to-wall revolution. We have found that the majority of passionate activists who hammer away at the old boundaries have given up family vacation, little league games, birthday dinners, evenings, weekends and lunch hours, gardening, reading, movies, and most other pastimes. We have a number of friends whose marriages or partnerships crumbled under the weight of their devotion to a dream. There are more newly single parents than we expected among our colleagues. We are frequently asked if it is possible to "have it all"—a full and satisfying personal life and a full and satisfying hard-working professional one. Our answer is: no. The price of excellence is time, energy, attention and focus. At the same time the energy, attention and focus could have gone toward enjoying your daughter's soccer game. Excellence is a high-cost item.[9]

Obsession with work is promoted as desirable in the excellent company. Peters and Austin go so far as to say that dedication to the company gives one a sense of purpose and allows one to recover self-respect. We question this attitude. Over time we have seen that what has been acceptable and desirable may indeed be a progressive and fatal disease of individuals *and* organizations.

ORGANIZATIONAL TRANSITION

We want to look now at another area, which is related to innovation, yet different: organizational transition. The focus here is on what happens to people in the innovation process. Significantly, the organizational transition material heralds a shift away from the rational-structural model to a process of considering the sociological and psychological effects of group events on the lives of people.

William Bridges, in his *Transition: Making Senses of Life Changes*, is a good example of this approach.[10] Bridges contends that transitions differ from organizational change in that change can proceed in a planned fashion whereas "transition is a three-part psychological process that extends over a long period of time and cannot be planned or managed with the same rational formula that works with change."[11] Bridges sees the three phases as (1) letting go of the old situation and the old identity that went with it, (2) going through a "neutral zone" between the old reality and the new reality, and (3) making a new beginning that is more than the "new start" required in a change. When Bridges applies his theories to organizational transitions, he sees people experiencing disengagement, disidentification, and disenchantment as they go through phase one, disorientation, disintegration, and discovery in phase two, and new visioning as they begin phase three.

One of our colleagues, who is an internal consultant in a Fortune 500 company, has followed the transition process closely as it affects employees. He finds Bridges's stages too mechanistic. Instead, he claims, in all transitions, whether in an organization or an individual's personal life, the seed of the new thing is planted very early on, usually when the current situation or relationship seems quite full. As a new idea grows, it develops within the existing situation, and often there are two things going on together, each claiming equal attention from employees. In an organization this is called "crazy time" because two different forms are making competing demands on people. Our friend does not find the neutral zone described by Bridges. Moreover, because change is constant, these transitions are always happening, and they are accompanied by feelings of loss and the need to grieve, even when the change is for the better. This suggestion that the idea is already there germinating supports our discovery that the *concept* of the addictive organization indeed fits our experience. We did not develop the idea; we discovered it when our perceptions and awareness developed to a point where we could see what was already there.

An article by Alan Sheldon, "Organizational Paradigms: A Theory of Organizational Change", describes the need for paradigmatic change when an organization finds itself "out of fit" with many aspects of its internal and external environment.[12] Paradigmatic change is a radical system shift that involves every level of functioning, not just a few adaptive responses. It also includes a change in the worldview of those within the company, often accompanied by mourning, because the old worldview is felt to be dying and must be abandoned.

Sheldon sees three kinds of paradigmatic shift: (1) a side-by-side overlap of the old and new paradigms, (2) a transformation in which the old paradigm is dead before the new is created, and (3) a supra-paradigm that superimposes the new on the old.

We find the organizational transition material very congruent with the work we do with people in organizations. It recognizes that structural changes are only part of the solution. People must always be considered, and their feelings and needs are part of the data that impacts the future. Also, the inclusion of grieving, which is felt in organizational transition, humanizes the company and keeps before it the realization that structures are not really external to the people involved. People and the processes they experience every day at all levels of their being are vastly important.

Along with our colleague, we question the neatness of Bridges's cycle of transition. We question whether this chronology takes place, while acknowledging that the feelings he describes do occur. The order he suggests may impose an artificial control on this process. Like Sheldon, we have seen the need for paradigmatic change. We question whether it is a real shift of paradigm if the driving force is merely the external environment, and we wonder if true system or paradigm shift is not first a change of attitude or worldview that also brings with it a different set of values.

LEADERSHIP

Everyone in the organizational field, it seems, is interested in the issue of leadership. We will survey a few representative works on this subject.

A recent book, *The Neurotic Organization,* takes a psychological perspective.[13] The authors describe five types of organizations in detail. They are the dramatic, depressive, paranoid, compulsive, and schizoid. Each of these types gets its character, and consequently many of its troubles, because the top executives exhibit one or more of these deep-seated neurotic styles. The neurotic styles of the executives then produce certain characteristic decisions and strategies of the company. Kets deVries and Miller conclude that some neurotic executive styles are actually compatible with the firm's environment. They also suggest a "healthy" mixture of neurotic styles can ensure corporate success.

Kets deVries and Miller have been helpful to us in our consulting practice because they have highlighted the amount of influence and power a top executive or key employee has on the whole climate of a company. Their research suggests that entire systems can take on the personality of the executive and be influenced by his or her behavior.

We have many questions about establishing neurotic behavior or a combination of neurotic styles as the norm for healthy organizational functioning. Even a mix of neurotic styles is still neurotic! We wonder if this kind of proposal indicates a more pervasive belief that the norm for organizations is dysfunctional behavior and whether this is accepted as "the way it is" in companies today. This certainly leads us to look at what has become "acceptable" in organizations and to question these assumptions.

A more practical, early "how-to" guide on leadership is Paul Hersey and Ken Blanchard's book on situational leadership.[14] Hersey and Blanchard are characteristic of the shifting context around the leadership issue. Historically the question has been, Are leaders born or made? Increasingly the answer is tending toward "made," and Hersey and Blanchard exemplify that school of thought.

They primarily focus on the context within which the leader operates. They have described four "styles" of leaders: telling, selling, participating, and delegating. Each of these styles describes a relationship the leader has to the other persons relative to the task at hand and the amount of personal interaction involved. The leader chooses the appropriate style based on his or her assessment of the maturity of the person with whom he or she is working. The assumption is that immature persons have to be "told," whereas highly self-motivated people can be delegated to.

Hersey and Blanchard have developed a simple yet powerful tool for understanding leadership. We are reminded by them that no one variety of leadership style is appropriate to all situations and that it is a mark of leadership to be flexible. We are less comfortable with the assumption that if the maturity level of workers is understood, they can be manipulated into acting a certain way and, moreover, move up a developmental ladder to greater maturity. We question this attitude, feeling that it feeds into an illusion of control and disrespect for workers. Furthermore, this approach, like so many others, is based upon a prescriptive model, which we think can be quite limiting.

Two other people-oriented books on leadership are Michael Maccoby's *The Leader* and Warren Bennis and Burt Nanus's *Leaders: The Strategies for Taking Charge.* [15] Maccoby selects six leaders in a variety of situations and follows them over time, interviewing them on factors that affect their style. Bennis and Nanus use a similar method, describing ninety leaders, from a Fortune 500 chairman to the conductor of a symphony orchestra. They isolate four strategies that outstanding leaders exhibit: they (1) pay attention through vision, (2) reach meaning through communication, (3) achieve trust, and (4) organize for innovative learning.

We appreciate that both books stress that leaders are people first. They recognize that when leaders are in touch with their own feelings and needs they are also more effective in their leadership role and they make risk-taking more attractive for themselves and others. Maccoby's example of a leader who became a team player—in fact, became so committed to this style of operation that he thought it a moral imperative for the company and his own continued health—is a powerful lesson. We wonder about the small changes that companies introduce that have life-changing effects on people and systems and, for some, lead to a radical shift in worldview. We see this happen with individuals more and more frequently. We ask ourselves, If it can happen with individuals, can it also happen in an entire system? We, indeed, believe it can, if we have more of the pieces to the larger puzzle.

The field called organizational development has been around for many years. It is interdisciplinary in nature, utilizing the insights of business, sociology, and psychology. It is a unique combination of scholarship that is applied to real-life situations, with the result that the practice of organizational development consistently feeds back into the theory. Lately there has been a "new kid on the block": organizational transformation.

ORGANIZATIONAL TRANSFORMATION

Organizational transformation is so new a field of study that it is difficult to be sure it will become a full-fledged field. Most of the authors we referred to thus far would see a need for organizational change if American companies are to become more productive and viable in the world. Organizational transformation, however, includes more in its survey of change affecting the corporate environment than most other approaches do.

In his preface to a collection of readings entitled *Transforming Work,* John Adams sets the following as the context in which organizations must operate.

If present world wide trends continue, by the year 2000 there will be 50% more people, 33% less top soil, 1.3 billion people experiencing malnutrition, a drastic shortage of clean water, as many as a million more species extinct, sufficient damage to the upper atmosphere to cause polar melts and radical climate changes, and 50% reduction in the forests of Asia, Africa and Latin America, and 40 nations with nuclear weapons. Furthermore, massive shifts and strains are developing in global economy. The organizations of the world, whether or not they are direct contributors to the problems such as these, will have to be part of the solution. The predominant mode of operating, focusing primarily on profit and return on investment, will have to give way to more global purposes if we are to survive.[16]

Organizational transformation incorporates this context as an indispensable environmental factor that must affect planning. Consequently, organizational transformation is not value free. It is vision led. We would say it is more than an alternative to organizational development, in that it has an appreciation of spirituality; indeed, it has a spiritual base as an explicit component.

Historically, organizational development first asked, How can organizations be more productive? Later, it asked, How can people be happier? Organizational transformation asks, How can the world be different as a result of the responsibility we take in it and our participation with it?

Other characteristics of organizational transformation are summarized by Peter Vaill in "Process Wisdom for a New Age." He says that organizational transformation is "being in the world with responsibility." This is a phenomenon rarely addressed by mainstream behavioral science, with its objectivist criteria for truth and relevance. There are three other clues as to what organizational transformation might be like. Organizational transformation is

(1) grounded in the actual existence that is life in organization, (2) a comfort and enjoyment of the openness of the human spirit to D. H. Lawrence's circumambient universe and an absence of an impulse to close off, to limit and to categorize fixedly, and (3) an understanding of human consciousness as our bridge to the world—not a radical subjectivity in which everything is relative, but a locating of awareness in the relationality of the human being through the people and things around it.[17]

We are excited about the possibility for organizational transformation. The characteristics Vaill outlines affirm our approach to groups. For example, for some time we have been aware that organizations were something other than they appeared or were made to appear. Because of the objectivist orientation of organizational development, we had been trained to be open only to certain types of information about organizations. Moreover, as consultants, we were expected to have prescriptions and packaged programs of solutions to problems.

One thing that remains to be seen with organizational transformation is whether the process of implementing this new approach to organizations will be any different from the former approach. This especially concerns the role of consultants. Is organizational transformation just another gimmick to sell the promise of higher productivity to organizations? Does it propose to do what it says—bring about a transformation of organizational life based on spiritual values? Does it formulate a system shift or subtly support existing systems? These are the concerns we have about organizational transformation, the questions we bring to it. It has great stated potential for true transformation. How can it do this without being coopted by the system?

As we opened ourselves to more information and relinquished fixed categories and assumptions, we began to see that some of the behaviors organizational development had categorized as "normal for organizations" were normal in the fixed system. If one viewed them from another perspective, they were seen for what they were—dysfunctional and addictive. This led us to realize that the worldview one holds circumscribes what problems are even seen and the context in which they are perceived. In order to see organizations from a different perspective, one must make a prior personal shift in worldviews. As this has happened in our lives, we have been forced into viewing the same phenomenon from a totally different perspective. When one makes a personal systems shift or changes worldview, facts emerge from the environment that were heretofore not seen and/or understood differently. It is not that they were not present, they were there all the time, yet frequently not seen at all.

THE PARADIGM SHIFT LITERATURE

Today there appears to be significant grass-roots ferment and a related, growing body of literature about something called the paradigm shift. In our work with groups and organizations, we have been aware that something qualitatively different appears to be happening both personally and culturally, something that has a life of its own. We want to consider, by way of summary, what some writers are saying about this paradigm shift as well as describe how their concepts have added to our awareness and brought a change in our own perceptions.

What are the origins of paradigm shift thinking, and more particularly, what does the concept of paradigm shift have to do with organizations? To answer the first question we have to turn to Thomas Kuhn, who in 1970 first delineated this idea.[18] He proposed that science advances both through normal science and through paradigmatic science. Normal science he saw as evolutionary and working within accepted rules. Paradigmatic science is the eruption of something that challenges and subsequently changes the rules. For Kuhn, a paradigm is a scientific theory, and it is more. A paradigm is a belief and explanation of observed phenomena that a specific community of people share. It is what they all believe about the way things are. A paradigm is both content (ideas) and process (method). Kuhn would say that it is both a way of going about the business of science and what the scientist sees. A paradigm is a superstructure that is a way of explaining what has been observed.

Crisis frequently precipitates the emergence of a new paradigm. Allen Sheldon, summarizing Kuhn, describes how this happens.

> When scientists find that old theories don't altogether work anymore, they begin to consider other alternatives, but they do not yet give up on the old theories. In fact, they will discard a scientific theory only if an alternative theory is available to take its place. So the decision to reject one paradigm simultaneously marks the decision to accept another. Crises help facilitate a fundamental paradigm shift. Simply by occurring, they call into disrepute the stereotypes which are adequate to deal with them and forcefully point out the need for a different model.[19]

An important characteristic of paradigms, one that affects the way we think about change, is that paradigmatic change is a shift between two worlds. It is whole and thoroughgoing. Therefore, paradigm shifts cannot be made incrementally, but occur all at once. It actually requires a radical conversion, rather than an ambling transition.

Kuhn's theory was one of the first, and surely one of the most influential, in establishing paradigm shift thinking. Though we find this concept helpful, it is also quite limited. From our perspective on the addictive organization, we would go one step further. We have come to question the underlying assumption of this theory. We have observed that a system in which things must build to a crisis and then shift radically is based on a worldview that is static and attempts to avoid change. Our sense is that there are other worldviews that are not recognized as valid because of the pervasiveness and rigidity of the current predominant view.

Perhaps in a "true" paradigm shift the shift is not to something new but to an an openness to see what is already present in the world yet not seen because it is occluded by the assumptions of the pervading worldview.

Kuhn's original observations were drawn from consideration of what was happening in the scientific community. We think he has isolated, as a by-product, an important development in the sciences. The scientific method, historically, was based on openness to all phenomena. Coincidentally, Kuhn has shown that science appears to have evolved into a static, closed system that no longer has the internal consistency of former times.

Marilyn Ferguson, in her best-selling *The Aquarian Conspiracy*, focused on the fact that the paradigm shift was not the invention of scientists, nor was it confined to the rhythm of science. "People everywhere were conspiring (from the Greek root: to breathe together) to move into a heretofore unnamed way of being which was holistic, healthy, cooperative, ecological, and spiritually based."[20] She acknowledges that this change was, indeed, emanating from the sciences, but also demonstrated evidence of it in every area of endeavor—business, education, religion, and medicine. Moreover, she contended, the paradigm shift was not a change imposed outside of individuals and society. It was an inner change that people experienced through meditation, personal crisis, and inner realizations; they then sought and found others whose specific experiences may have been different yet were recognizable as similar paradigm shifts.

David Bohm's influence on the paradigm shift discussions is probably more limited than Ferguson's, yet his contribution is of great importance.[21] Bohm is a physicist who has begun to look at physics and science from a totally different perspective from the traditional Newtonian scientific worldview. We believe that Bohm's particularly important contribution to the paradigm discussion is his insight that the world is a hologram. Briefly, an example of a hologram is what is achieved when a laser beam projects an image in three-dimensional likeness into space and then onto a photographic plate.

What excited hard science and social science alike was the nature of the projected image. It was a hologram: if the image was broken into separate pieces, the individual pieces held the entire image. Thus a hologram contains all the pieces, and the individual pieces contain the entire hologram. Or, in nonscientific terms, the individual is the whole, the whole is the individual. Paradoxically, the hologram suggests that things can be simultaneously different and the same.

Bohm took the concept of hologram further into the concept of holo-movement, a description of a process, that we live in a nonstatic universe. In so doing, he opens up the possibility of revolutionizing the way we view ourselves and the world by offering an alternative to a static, control-oriented, objective, scientific worldview.

Recent brain research (by Karl Pribrim) suggests that the human brain does indeed function as a hologram, "a holo-movement." This means that we are now beginning to look anew at the ancient Mayan and Egyptian sciences as holographic, which adds a new dimension to our understanding. The brain and the individual both are the universe and vice versa.

The concept of the hologram was also exciting news for the social sciences, students of organizations, and theologians. It gave form to something many social researchers had been working on for years—the meaning of the interconnectedness of behavior and lives, the ecological-organic view of the world and of groups.

What, you may ask, do esoteric brain researchers, holograms, and paradigm shifts in the sciences have to do with organizations? A lot, say some respected organizational consultants. One of them, Charles Hampden-Turner, contends that the same issues of paradigm shifts and the proper model of the brain (i.e., left-brain, right-brain dominance) are being fought out in corporations at this very moment.[22] Turner would say that issues such as the crisis in corporate planning, the role of government in making industrial policy, the crisis of falling productivity, the cultural economies of Japan and the United States, and the economy in the year 2000 are all caught up in paradigm wars and are only soluble by paradigm cooperation.

In an article called "Is There a New Paradigm? A Tale of Two Concepts," Turner establishes that there are at least two paradigms already in existence, and perhaps even more. Even more significant is his insistence that paradigm II (the new emerging paradigm) not become an object of worship. He proposes that its processes, patterns, and relationships not be approached in the style of the former paradigm. His concern is that "wholeness will become a thing, rather than a process of reconciling." Turner warns that

> the values of paradigm II are not a grab bag, they cannot be seized or appropriated, they come by indirection, by going the full circle, development by way of concern for others, conviction earned by doubt, emotional security through vulnerability. It is quite a different world than the pop-psych supermarket and will require of us nothing less than a fundamental change.[23]

Our experience of organizational change is that many people in organizations are looking for a "fix," both personally and organizationally. The "fix" is any process or thing that the individual or group can get busy about so as not to face their own process, learn from it, and make full-scale changes. The former paradigm based on objectivist science provided fixes in the form of answers. With Turner, we see that a paradigm shift is a move away from the certainty of the right answers to a process of transformation and a world of the unknown. In some ways it is what theologians have called "a leap into the void."

We conclude our survey of paradigm shift issues by referring to a creative and scholarly contributor to the discussion, Morris Berman. Berman has published an important book, *The Reenchantment of the World,* in which he argues persuasively that we are looking at the demise of a major worldview.[24] He says this worldview is becoming entropic, eating itself up, destroying itself, that it is based on logical positivism and empiricism and it is what we have known as the basic scientific method. Berman sees the scientific worldview as being a nonparticipatory model based on making the self and the other and the world objects to be observed. The self is removed from participating with the self, with others, and with the world in which we live. Berman believes we must develop some alternative to this objectifying process, and he proposes the development of what he calls a "participatory consciousness." What are the keys for organizations in these paradigm considerations? We are seeing that many organizations function under the myth of objectivity, a myth that seems to be inherited from the scientific worldview. Along with this belief in the supposed superiority of objectivity is a tendency to worship the logical and rational. As consultants we are frequently met with the request to be "objective outsiders" who will help design structures to "take care of our problems." Since the problems are holographic, that is, in the people as well as the system, no reliance on the perfect structure will resolve the problems, even minimally. Underlying such a worldview is the illusion of control, which proposes that somehow we can make anything work out the way we want it. We are seeing that such thinking is directly related to a paradigm of objectivity in which, as Berman points out, we are no longer participants in our own experience or in the world around us. We find this illusion and concomitant detachment frequently in organizations. People are estranged from themselves, others, and the world. They do not have available information from all three spheres, which would support creative decision making, for example. Moreover, though few organizations would claim that they believe the world is static and unchanging, their mode of operating indicates that they want a static world and believe it is possible to create one. All this leads us to ponder the pervasiveness of a system that is discredited by the paradigm writers as dying and on its way out.

WOMEN'S WRITING

To bypass the influence of women's literature would be to ignore a major social change movement of this century, the women's movement, and not to be true to our own experience as women. Thus, we consider some themes here and acknowledge their influence as one major force that contributed to our ability to see the organization as addict. We found these themes in women's science fiction and fantasy, fiction, books about women in organizations, and women's nonfiction systems writing.

FANTASY AND SCIENCE FICTION

Some representative writers of fantasy and science fiction are Marion Zimmer Bradley, Charlotte Perkins Gilman, Carol Hill, Ursula LeGuin, and Anne McCaffrey.[25] These are all women, whose novels we read for pleasure and in reading them discovered some fascinating and thought-provoking ideas. One thing they all have in common is that they have developed worlds entirely out of their own imaginations. Another common theme is that they all create entirely different worlds from the one in which we live. The worlds they create generally have feminist values. In Bradley's *Thendara House* women are women-identified in guilds resembling abbeys. Women have the power of the matrix, a tool for communication, which is used for healing, as a power source, for time and space travel, and psychic energies. We see in these books, societies in which there is female leadership, where authority is shared equally by men and women and where roles are not prescribed based on gender or if they are, women have a major role and their talents are highly valued by the culture.

Bradley, LeGuin, and McCaffrey weave societies in which there are other levels of information besides the logical and rational. Their characters use telepathy and go into cosmic states of consciousness. All of this is legitimated, highly valued and used in their society and science, not just by the privileged few, but by all.

The inhabitants of these books are frequently at war with others and the repressive systems they war against have characteristics akin to the society in which we live.

McCaffrey and Hill take us on space travel on conveyances as diverse as dragons, rocket boosters, and roller skates. While traveling easily into past and future times, they take us deeper inside their heroines to new concepts of personal power, the value of self-awareness and new insight.

Relationships are important in these books and every type abounds. The rigid sexual boundaries of our society disappear. Men relate physically in friendship, partnership and telepathically with other men, with women, and with both men and women, as do women. Families are filled with old, young, foster children, and wayfarers. In Anne McCaffrey's books, people have a special relationship with their dragons with whom they bond for life. Ursula LeGuin invites us to sympathize with our Sister, Mt. St. Helens when she erupted. She writes on the essential female characteristics of Mt. St. Helens which will not be tamed, predicted, controlled, or analyzed into submissiveness. She is uniquely a woman blowing her top.

For us, immersion in this type of literature opened us to an awareness of how far ranging the alternative system can be. Moreover, it showed us that there already exists a widespread knowledge of alternative systems. Even if this acknowledgement is underground in women's fantasy literature, it still fortunately offers alternative perspectives. We felt a ready identification with these other worlds, as well as support and affirmation for our own efforts to identify other paradigms in organizations.

FICTION

Fiction writers like Margaret Atwood, Mary Gordon, Keri Hume, Toni Morrison, Gloria Naylor, May Sarton, and Alice Walker gave us information and perspective on this culture from those who had stepped outside it through short story and fiction.[26] They put before us a powerful awareness of the exploitation of women and racial ethnic people. Gloria Naylor shows us blacks who have "made it" in the culture where the cost is essentially losing their souls to the system they have longed to emulate. Margaret Atwood's heroine in *The Edible Woman* serves her fiance a cake in the form of a woman with the message, "Eat this because I won't let you devour me."

Many of these writers delve into themes which are intensely personal and subjective and then use these microcosms as a mirror of the world, giving credence to the feminist saying, "the personal is political and the political is personal." Mary Gordon in *Men and Angels* treats motherhood as a dangerous and necessary "career." Keri Hume creates an almost mystical context for child abuse and domestic violence, while demonstrating that addictions are key to both. May Sarton's *Kinds of Love* uses suicide as social blame and release. Morrison and Walker view the white culture from an external perspective while establishing that black culture need not reference itself to the white system.

Most of these authors do an explicit critique of a white male, or patriarchal system, while expanding our imaginations with varieties of responses possible in such a system. For some of them there is hope and self-affirmation, for others, desperation. However, no one remains unaffected.

These writings gave us a fuller perspective on our own culture as well as that of others. Continual immersion in these books resulted in a raising of our consciousness to the effects of living in this system. This validated our perceptions of the existence of different realities and systems and helped us focus what we were observing in organizations.

WOMEN IN ORGANIZATIONS AND MANAGEMENT

Next we turn to women in organizations, books written by Harragan, Kanter, Hart, and others.[27] Harragan says in *Games Mother Never Taught You* that there is a corporate mindset, a climate. If women are going to "make it" in the corporate world, they need to learn the rules of this game and then play as well as or better than men. Books written more recently, like *Success and Betrayal: The Crisis of Women in Corporate America*, contend that even when women learn the system, they still do not "make it." Kanter shows in *Men and Women of the Corporation* that the introduction of significant numbers of women in formerly male-dominated roles reduces stereotyping, but does not necessarily change the operational style of the company. This relates to statements in *Success and Betrayal* that women are now beginning to leave corporations because they realize that they are not going to make it to the top and they really have not been influential in changing the climate of corporations to make them more humanistic and healthy. Recent studies show that these women are leaving corporations to return to homemaker roles and/or start their own businesses where they can be more influential in determining the climate of the organization. As Fassel has investigated all female work groups, she finds that the white male system flourishes in these groups except where all members make an explicit commitment to another style of operating.

The value of these types of books to us is that they recognize that women in corporations are a significant entity and furthermore, that there is a corporation system (which may be a corporation reflection of the society), which is different from the world many women and minorities inhabit. There is also, in several of these books, the assumption that this corporate system is worth learning. In fact, the key to success is to learn the system, to emulate it. In a large measure, there is little evidence that women are affecting these systems, and more recent research seems to indicate that women, like men, are being eaten up by them.

We know from our work with organizations that the addictive process is pervasive, contagious, and has generally remained unnamed and therefore unaddressed in the society and organizations. The process perpetuates a denial system which makes it all the more difficult to see what is going on in oneself and in organizations. Unfortunately, many of these books support women's remaining in and adjusting to a dysfunctional and destructive system. We believe this observation supports our contention of how widespread the problem is and how everyone can be caught up in it, even when, by definition, they cannot get the supposed benefits of being coopted into the organization.

WOMEN'S BOOKS ON ALTERNATIVE SYSTEMS

Lastly we consider some books on alternative systems, books whose exclusive purpose is to describe other ways of being in the universe. A representative sample is Daly's *Beyond God the Father,* Gilligan's *In a Different Voice,* Dodson-Grey's *Patriarchy as a Conceptual Trap,* Rich's *Lies, Secrets and Silences,* and Schaef's *Women's Reality.* [28] These books say unequivocally that there is a white, patriarchal male system. They clearly state that the dominant system is destructive to people and the universe and that there are other realities. Daly shows that our concepts of God are socially conditioned by the church and theology and are inventions of men. Gilligan challenges our theories of moral development, showing that women approach moral questions differently, and though different from men, have high levels of moral development. Schaef believes there is a white male system that operates out of four myths and continues to exist because we all cooperate with it. Rich believes that even our thought patterns are in the language of a male system that has rewarded lies, secrets, and silences on the part of women. Dodson-Grey follows Rich with her theory that patriarchy is a mode of thought that has influenced our judgment about what is worth knowing and how it is known.

By the very fact that these authors describe the existing system, they imply that it is only one reality. There are other realities, as Schaef says, women's reality, black reality, native American reality, and so on. It is not that these other realities do not exist, it is that they are not valued and their insights are not recognized, used, or validated in the society. In fact, the society basically denies the very existence of these other realities.

All of these writers feel that long immersion in the white male system is unhealthy, personally and universally. All of them call for a change, and they suggest alternatives based on a more inclusive model that is concerned for the life of the individual, the environment, and the planet.

In connection with these writers, it should be noted that there is an increasing number of men who perceive the same problem the women describe. Jed Diamond, Ken Druck, Herb Goldberg, to name a few, are heralding the same concerns and issues while focusing upon the needs of men.[29]

Overall, these systems writers alerted us to other options and invited us to see the white male system for what it is: a system, not reality. We began to see that the purpose of a "raised consciousness" is not to impose reality but to be less oblivious to what is already present. The issue is not a new vision, but to see what is already there and has always been there, and see it from a fuller perspective. The problem was more one of "for those who have eyes to see, let them see, for those who have ears to hear, let them hear." We know that being caught in an addictive system, or any dysfunctional organizational system, limits seeing, hearing, and knowing. These writers have articulated other systems; this offers the possibility of options.

At the same time we were immersing ourselves in the literature of the authors just mentioned, and many others, we were also working with increasing numbers of women's groups and were personally involved as participants in women's groups. As a result of this involvement, we began to live out of a different paradigm, which we have called the living process system. The living process system gave us the needed distance from existing systems to offer us a perspective, a place from which to see the dominant system for what it is, a system about which we have a choice.

The next piece of the puzzle came from our growing awareness about and our own involvement in the field of addictions.

ADDICTIONS

Our knowledge of addictions came from reading the literature in the field and uniquely from our own personal experience as recovering co-dependents. By recognizing the disease of co-dependence in our lives we had to begin a program of treatment and to develop a working relationship with the twelve-step program of Alcoholics Anonymous. Our reading in the field and our recovery process supported each other, and wove a powerful experiential-intellectual base for our ongoing work with organizations.

PERSONAL INVOLVEMENT

It is important to note here that the really vital thrust of our learning truly came from personal involvement in recovery from our co-dependence. This is because recovery in Alcoholics Anonymous and related AA programs (Al-Anon, Overeaters Anonymous, Narcotics Anonymous, Debtors Anonymous, etc.) ultimately means entering upon a personal systems shift. Basically, for the alcoholic (or any addictive person) it means moving out of the addictive system, which is a nonliving system, into a system of recovery, of choosing to be fully alive. The AA model calls for a paradigm shift like what we described earlier, a shift in an entire worldview.

The personal system shift we entered into was not available to us through objective study of the literature on addictions or through systematic training in the field. To make this shift and to "know it" at a level other than the rational, we had to *do* our recovery process. Hence we moved from a position of depending upon learning from authorities and literature to a reliance on our own experience as the central focus for our learning. We became involved in a *participatory* system. Along the way we discovered that the writers who were most exciting and relevant to us were those who were affirming and articulating what we were already finding through our own experience. As the process of personal recovery progressed, elaborated by reading in the addictions field, we began to move beyond our previous selves. What initially began as our personal exploration not only became the foundation for perceiving ourselves and our families differently, it also began to affect the way we perceived the organizations in which we lived and with which we worked.

Ultimately we began to have a different perspective on the entire social system.

As we did our personal journey and immersed ourselves in the literature, a third thing was happening in the society at large. There began to be a growing awareness of the epidemic proportion of the problem of addiction. Addictions treatment came "out of the closet" due, in part, to various celebrities going for treatment. Reagan's war on drugs and the drug and alcohol information in the schools brought the problem to the immediate forum. A problem that had been prevalent, yet hidden in the past, was now front and center.

LITERATURE ON ADDICTION

When we turned to literature in the field of addiction, we found a massive body of work in the scientific and medical research journals; primarily this literature investigates alcoholism. However, when we search for books that are serious treatments of the social problems of addictions and the underlying addictive process, or when we look for the systems implications of the disease of addictions, we find ourselves turning to a different kind of literature. Clearly, we are at the beginning of the escalation of this problem. Nevertheless, there are some representative books we can consult.

There are four areas in the literature we survey here: the disease of alcoholism, addictions and family systems, adult children of alcoholics and co-dependents, and wider system perspective.

In the first area, the disease of alcoholism, is the basic book of Alcoholics Anonymous, *Alcoholics Anonymous*, which is referred to by people in the twelve-step program as "the Big Book."[30] This is the book that contains the Twelve Steps and Twelve Traditions and is the most widely used in all recovery and treatment programs. All other twelve-step programs (Narcotics, Overeaters, Debtors, Sexual, etc.) use the Big Book and their own materials geared to their specific addiction. The Big Book contains a description of the dynamics of the disease and a program that cannot be understood simply by reading it. To do this "program" requires personal involvement. Another excellent book describing the addictive disease is Vernon Johnson's *I'll Quit Tomorrow.*[31] We believe it is one of the best introductory books in the field. It describes the disease, the characteristics of an alcoholic, and the process of intervention and treatment. For someone just beginning this investigation, Johnson is excellent. The important thing to see about these writings is that they are not just describing the specific disease of alcoholism, they are describing a much broader syndrome.

On addiction and family systems, Sharon Wegscheider-Cruse and Robert Subby are representative.[32] Wegscheider-Cruse's book *Another Chance: Help and Hope for the Alcoholic Family* makes important contributions to the field by showing that all family members are affected by the disease of alcoholism. She describes roles children take in such families (the hero child, the scapegoat, the lost child, the mascot) and the way these roles are played out in adult life. Coming from a family systems background, Wegscheider-Cruse is able to detail the important impact the disease has on an entire system. Robert Subby also comes out of a family systems perspective. He focuses more on the rules that are established in alcoholic families. He identifies nine, including Don't talk, Don't feel, Don't rock the boat, Be strong, good, right, and perfect. Subby concludes that members of the alcoholic family are co-dependents whose emotional, psychological, and behavioral condition is a result of prolonged exposure to repressive rules.

People who grow up in untreated alcoholic families, or in any family in which there is a nonrecovering addict, are called adult children of alcoholics (ACOA) or co-dependents. Janet Woititz investigates this phenomenon in her best-selling book *Adult Children of Alcoholics*.[33] She describes the characteristics of co-dependent adult children: they guess at what normal is, stay in relationships beyond the time they should leave, are super-responsible or super-irresponsible, judge themselves without mercy, don't know what they feel, and so on. Woititz has also clarified for us that adult children have a unique disease with its own properties. It is not the disease of the alcoholic; basically it is the other side of a disease of the alcoholic though at some level is the *same* disease, since they are both outgrowths of the underlying addictive process. Claudia Black's book *It Will Never Happen to Me* was an early book on the theme of adult children of alcoholics.[34]

Wegscheider-Cruse initially defined a co-dependent as a person who is (1) in a love or marriage relationship with an alcoholic, (2) has one or more alcoholic parents or grandparents, or (3) grew up in an emotionally repressive family. By Wegscheider-Cruse's estimation, this amounts to 96 percent of the population. Other authors would say that a co-dependent is not just someone who grew up in an alcoholic family; they recognize the same effects in any family that is dysfunctional and/or has any kind of untreated addiction, which is, as we believe, most people in an addictive society.

These authors have shown us the pervasiveness of the problem of addiction. By not treating the disease of the family members, behaviors arise that cause the family to develop its own disease, co-dependence. The disease of co-dependence needs to be treated. Family members should start recovery, or they reproduce dysfunctional systems in other settings. Essentially, the fact is that if you are not recovering, you are part of the problem. The authors mentioned limit their analysis to the family system. In fact, it would seem that they see the family as the primary system.

We recognize the family as an important system, and we see it as only one system. We participate in a variety of systems all our lives. It is necessary to widen the analysis beyond the family, or we could delude ourselves into thinking that treating the family is all that is necessary for recovery.

Charles Whitfield and Anne Wilson Schaef recognize the need to widen our perspective beyond the family. Whitfield feels that co-dependence influences "communities, businesses and other institutions, states and countries."[35] Whitfield, a medical doctor, also discusses the power of co-dependent and addicted medical people and social workers, who have their own need for treatment. He says that those closest to the disease often develop the most sophisticated "con," which in turn protects their own addiction for years. Anne Wilson Schaef, more than anyone else writing in the field, goes beyond specific social systems and into the very system in which we live. In two books, *Co-Dependence: Misunderstood, Mistreated* and *When Society Becomes an Addict,* she argues that the problem is not just individuals who are multiply addicted or families who are co-dependent.[36] Schaef says there is a generic addictive process that underlies all the various addictions. Indeed, our society itself is an addictive system and acts exactly like an individual addict in the way it functions and the processes it sets up. Thus the theory of an addictive personality clouds the issue. The problem is not that there are people running around with addictive personalities; there exists an addictive process that underlies an addictive system, and it surrounds and influences all of us.

All of those writing in the addictions field agree that this is a disease of enormous power, that it is insidious and pervasive. Some of them differ in their analysis; however, most agree on the characteristics of addicts and co-dependents. From personal experience we could verify much of what we read in these books, and we began to see more.

Because of our involvement in our own recovery and in the recovery of others, we began to develop a different perspective on some of the issues we were seeing in organizations. We went back to writers like Berman who are calling for a participatory system, and we began to see the implications of what it means to say that the system in which we function now is not reality but an illusionary system that functions like an addict. Berman claimed that the underlying assumptions of the scientific worldview caused the gradual death of such a paradigm and of those who tried to exist in it. We discovered that the same characteristics of Berman's outlined as a scientific method paradigm were also the characteristics of an addict in an addictive system.

Concurrently, we became aware of a major social transformational movement that has many members, is very powerful, is making a great impact on the culture, and is little discussed. This movement is the twelve-step program. As we began to talk openly about our respect for and involvement in the twelve-step program, we discovered droves of people coming "out of the closet" and found not only that large numbers of people participate in these programs but also some were very influential people as well. This indeed is more of a force in our society than we had realized.

SUMMARY

All of the fields in which we read began to come together for us in a new way. From organizational development we saw the strain in companies as groups grappled with issues of participation, innovation, and transition; clearly, the external environment and the demands of consumers were pushing organizations to change. From paradigm shift studies, we were impressed with the scope and scale of the kind of shift that was taking place. It was thorough, taking place and at all levels of the society. Women's writing showed us that the system in which we live is not the only reality: many other realities exist and have always been there. The addictions field finally gave us the missing piece. Synthesizing the work of writers in this field and our own experience, we saw that the characteristics of the individual addict were also the characteristics of the system in which we live. It is indeed a hologram.

Now we have the missing piece we were looking for and one that we see absent from other writings on organizations. If it is true we live in a holographic universe, then it becomes obvious that the system functions as an addict and reflects the addictive characteristics of the individual, while the individual reflects the addictive process of the system. Actually, neither reflects the other, for they are not a mirror, they *are* the other. Next we saw that we had to be open to accepting that organizations are developed by and inhabited by individuals who are also part of a hologram and that these organizations also serve to support the society in which they exist, which is an addictive society. Consequently, if we are to be able to understand organizations and to work creatively with them, we have to be open to the ways the organizations themselves are the same as the addictive society. Individuals function the same way as the organization they inhabit. Organizations function the same way as the system they inhabit, and the system is made up of the individuals in the organizations. We do indeed have our hologram.

We think it is important to say here that at no time did we approach the organizations with whom we worked with the idea of the organization as addict. Once awareness had been raised by the influences just described, we began to view the dynamics of the organization from a new perspective and be open to information that had not been available to us previously because we simply did not see it. (We believe we probably would not have seen it without the experiences we have described.) Because of this new perspective, we began to categorize and group the information we gathered differently. This led us to the startling awareness that organizations themselves function as addicts, and because they are not aware of this fact of their functioning, become key building blocks in an addictive society, even when this dramatically contradicts their espoused mission or reason for existence. Addictive organizations are the infrastructure of the addictive society. They are the "glue" that perpetuates addictive functioning on the societal level. Slowly we began to see that some of the very ideas and approaches that were effective with individual addicts and families could be successfully applied to organizations. We began to see more clearly how organizations can be helped toward recovery and transformation.

II

THE ADDICTIVE
SYSTEM—TERMS AND
CHARACTERISTICS

The Addictive System—Terms and Characteristics

There is a massive literature describing addictions and the characteristics of addictions. We referred to a very few examples in Section I. Here we intend to develop some general concepts in order to set the discussion of the addictive organization in its proper context. First, let us look at some terms: addiction, system, addictive system, and co-dependence. Anne Wilson Schaef has done some of the most current and thorough work in this area (see *When Society Becomes an Addict* for a complete treatment of the addictive system); we rely heavily on her writing for our approach to these terms.

ADDICTION

An addiction is any substance or process that has taken over our lives and over which we are powerless. It may or may not be a physiological addiction. An addiction is any process or substance that begins to have control over us in such a way that we feel we must be dishonest with ourselves or others about it. Addictions lead us into increasing compulsiveness in our behavior. Schaef says that an addiction is anything we feel we have to lie about. If there is something we are not willing to give up in order to make our lives fuller and more healthy, it probably can be classified as an addiction.

SUBSTANCE AND PROCESS ADDICTION

Addictions fall into two major categories: substance addictions and process addictions. The substance addictions are ingestive; substances are taken into the body. All the mood-altering chemicals, some of which lead to increased physical dependence, are addictive substances. The most prevalent addictive substances are alcohol, drugs, caffeine, nicotine, salt, sugar, and food. The concept of process addictions refers to a series of activities or interactions that "hook" a person, or on which a person becomes dependent. The common process addictions are work, sex, money, gambling, religion, relationships, and certain types of thinking. Actually, any process can be used addictively. For example, Schaef points out that even worry can be a process addiction.[1] She describes a client who worried constantly. She worried when she felt good and she worried when she felt bad. When she had nothing to worry about, she felt lost. Worry had become an addictive process for her. It had a life of its own such that the actual content of the worry was not the issue; it was the act of worrying that was important in this woman's life.

The point is anything can be used addictively, whether it be a substance or a process. This is because the purpose or function of an addiction is to put a buffer between ourselves and our awareness or feelings. An addiction serves to numb us so that we are out of touch with what we know and what we feel. Moreover, we often get so taken up with the addiction—an addictive relationship, for example—that we have no energy for or awareness of other aspects of our life.

Once we consulted with a financial institution where there was perpetual conflict among the employees. One of the practices in this business was to provide lots of food and alcoholic drinks during the staff meetings. The manager believed that socializing during the meetings helped people loosen up and act less hostile toward one another. The actual effect of the alcohol and food was to take the edge off the conflicts to such an extent that the manager could never surface them and focus upon what the employees were feeling. Moreover, the alcohol affected their ability to pay close attention to what was being said and the issues being raised. Conversations became confused, resulting in the conflicts being more submerged and, therefore, more intense. In our beginning attempts to work with the group, we insisted that no food or alcohol be available at meetings, hoping that everyone could have a more direct experience of the intensity of the conflict. We believed as long as the group was out of touch with their emotions around an issue, they had no way of understanding its meaning in their work together. This strategy was effective, and we were able to surface and work through the issues involved.

Substance and process addictions usually have a meaning beyond the personal. The society in which we live needs addictions, and its very essence fosters addictions. It fosters addictions because the best-adjusted person in the society is the person who is not dead and not alive, just numb, a zombie. When you are dead you are not able to do the work of the society. When you are fully alive, you are constantly saying no to many of the processes of the society: the racism, the polluted environment, the nuclear threat, the arms race, drinking unsafe water, and eating carcinogenic foods. Thus, it is in the interests of the society to promote those things that "take the edge off," get us busy with our "fixes," and keep us slightly "numbed out" and zombielike. Consequently, the society itself not only encourages addictions, it functions as an addict.

SYSTEM

By system we mean an entity that comprises both content (ideas, roles, and definitions) and processes (ways of doing things), and that is complete in itself. A system is made up of parts, and the system is larger than the sum of the parts. A system often has a life of its own distinct from the lives of the individuals within it. A number of our clients who work in large corporations have observed that the corporation itself is a being that is greater than the composite of all the workers. This life or system has a tradition, a way of doing things, unwritten norms, and expectations passed on within the system. The system existed before the present employees and will go on after them.

Systems contain within themselves entire worldviews. They are internally consistent paradigms, and the paradigms are expected to make sense of everything that happens within them. They explain our experience, and they validate our actions. The system will utilize information differently depending on how open or closed it is. In closed systems, information that cannot be processed within the existing paradigm will not be allowed in or recognized. By definition, it simply does not exist. Open systems take in new information, they espouse flexibility as one of the characteristics of their system, and they are open to new information as a way to initiate change.

All systems call for behaviors and processes from those within the system that are consistent with the system. Systems subtly and explicitly reward people for exhibiting these behaviors.

Recently we were doing an organizational assessment in a mid-sized company. The president was discussing a man in the company who had been a powerful and charismatic leader. He was well liked by his staff. He had just resigned, however. When we asked the reason for his leaving, the president said, "Oh, he got a divorce, and we can't have that." There is nothing in the formal personnel procedures that says you cannot be divorced and be a vice-president in this company. But in this system, it is the unspoken yet accepted "rule."

ADDICTIVE SYSTEM

An addictive system is first of all a closed system. It is closed because it presents very few options to the individual in terms of roles and behaviors, or even the thinking and perceptions a person can recognize and pursue. Basically, an addictive system calls for addictive behaviors. It invites the person into the processes of addiction and addictive thinking patterns. Even if we ourselves are not addicted to a substance or a process (which is unusual in this society), since the addictive system exists as the norm for the society its processes are always available to be tapped into by anyone at any time. It is here that the notion of the hologram is useful. The addictive system is the same as the individual addict, and the individual addict is the same as the addictive system. In other words, the addictive system has all the characteristics of the individual addict, and the individual addict has the characteristics of the addictive society. Consequently, by virtue of the fact that we live in this system, we carry many of the characteristics of the addictive system unless we are actively recovering from it by means of a system shift.

CHARACTERISTICS OF ADDICTION

The addictive system operates from the same characteristics that individual addicts have routinely exhibited. The major defense mechanism of the addictive system is *denial,* which supports a closed system. If something does not exist, it simply does not have to be considered. Corporations frequently say, "We have a minor problem, but certainly not a major one." We are having a sales slump, but it is only temporary. The alcoholic says, "I am not an alcoholic. I may have a small drinking problem, and I may overdo it a bit on weekends or under stress, but I do not have a severe problem." Denial prevents us from coming to terms with what is going on before our very eyes. When we will not let ourselves see or know what is happening, we pose no threat to the continuation of a dysfunctional system, and we perpetuate a dishonest system.

Confusion is another characteristic of the addictive system; alcoholic family systems are filled with confusion. Everyone spends inordinate amounts of time trying to figure out what is going on. Family members, in their attempts to control the behavior of the alcoholic, fall all over themselves and one another trying to predict what will happen next and how to deal with it. This leads to in massive confusion.

Confusion plays a vital role in the addictive system. Confusion prevents us from taking responsibility; it keeps us ignorant of what is really going on; it keeps us busy trying to figure out what is happening; and ultimately it keeps us powerless to get what we need out of the system. In some organizations, confusion is the norm. These organizations thrive on crisis and hardly know how to function when things are "normal." Also present is a type of confused thinking that is characteristic of the thinking we find in an addictive system.

Self-centeredness is a prominent characteristic of addicts and the addictive system. This is partially because getting the "fix" becomes the center of an addict's life. Everything else is overshadowed. The self-centeredness of the addictive system is not only selfishness, it is also making the self the center of the universe. Everything that happens is thus perceived as either an assault on or an affirmation of the self. It is "for" or "against" the self. Developing this definition further, martyrdom, guilt, and shame are also self-centered activities.

On a national level, we can see self-centeredness operating in our foreign policy. Everything happening in the world is seen as either for or against the United States. Even the actions of nonaligned nations are viewed within the framework of our interests.

Dishonesty is certainly a key aspect of the addictive system. Anyone who has been around an active addict knows that he or she is a master liar. Active addicts have perfected the "con" to a fine art. Schaef details three levels of lying by addicts. First, addicts lie to themselves. The purpose of this lying is to stay out of touch with what they are feeling and what they know and need. Then, addicts lie to people around them, and by so doing, create a confusing and dishonest family system. Finally, they lie to the world at large. One example of this is "putting up a good front" to the community.

The addictive system fosters dishonesty at every turn. We have interviewed many executives who have been told that if they did not learn to be dishonest, they would never "make it" in the company. We are subtly expected to cheat on our taxes or to take advantage of a mistake on our restaurant tab. We dress for success because wearing the uniform suggests we can do the job. There is a belief that if the "package" is convincing, we can hide behind it regardless of our qualifications. Women in management training are told to hide their feelings and not say what they think. We are taught, when in doubt, never show it. Always act "as if we know what we are doing."

Dishonesty appears to be the cornerstone of our political system, as demonstrated in the latest technique: disinformation. A conversation we recently overheard on an airplane illustrates this perfectly: "I told Judge ———'s lawyers, 'Work as hard as you can, but be sure you lose.'" Dishonesty has so become the norm that we all expect not to be able to believe what we are told in advertising, product guarantees, construction bids, or in business in general.

Perfectionism is another interesting characteristic of the addictive system. One would never expect to find that addicts are perfectionists, but they are. They are obsessed with not being good enough, not doing enough, and not being able to be perfect as the system defines perfect. The tendency toward perfectionism is considered a major stumbling block to the successful treatment of an active addict. Addicts use their perfectionism as a way of seeing themselves as bad people trying to become good, instead of sick people trying to get well.

In the addictive system, perfectionism means always knowing the answers, being first with the solution, and never making a mistake. This is different from striving to make a high-quality product. The addictive system actually assumes that it is *possible* to be perfect as defined by the system (which is at best an abstract, God-like definition); consequently, it expects the impossible from everyone.

Those who buy into the perfectionism of the addictive system are always experiencing themselves as failures. Mistakes are unacceptable in the perfectionistic system, and when they do occur, they are quickly denied or covered up. In this system, mistakes are not valid material for learning; they are indicative of imperfection. This is an unfortunate view, because "failures" are often rich sources of data for individuals and groups.

The addictive system also operates out of a *scarcity model.* In this system, there is an abiding belief that there is simply not enough to go around. The addict is always trying to get "more" of something—his or her addictive substance, money, time, or love, for example. This frantic pursuit of more builds because the addictive substance (or process) of choice eventually stops packing its original punch. The "fix" of the addictive substance or process is never enough, because it is an attempt to do something that is not possible: fill us up from the outside. No fix will ever do that, so we are constantly dissatisfied.

The scarcity model in the addictive system is a model driven by consideration of quantity. It comes out of a quantitative mentality. Frequently, moreover, it is an attempt to measure things that are not quantifiable. We want more love, attention, affection, and time. We begin to look to outward symbols for inner assurance.

The system in which we live operates on the same scarcity principles. The addictive system is constantly in search of more armaments, a larger gross national product, or more international influence. At every shareholder meeting, the bottom line focus is measured by getting bigger in one way or another. A major preoccupation of the addictive system is *control,* or more accurately, *the illusion of control.* The addict and the addict's family are constantly preoccupied with controlling one another. The family tries to control the addict; the addict's behavior is controlling the family; the co-dependent spouse is trying to avoid being controlled; and everyone is going crazy.

We call this the *illusion* of control because none of us can truly control anything. However, the addictive system harbors a belief that it is possible to control everything; in fact, the illusion of control begins with the addict's attempt to control the self with a substance or a process. By taking a drug or drink, addicts believe they can avoid dealing with what they are feeling, thinking, needing, wanting, or knowing. From this first illusion of control, they believe they can then control what others are feeling as well. Whenever a system is operating out of the illusion of control, it is an addictive system by definition.

Because the illusion of control is so pervasive, addicts have to deal with the reality of *frozen feelings*. In addiction circles, this refers to the fact that most addicts are almost totally out of touch with their feelings, intuition, and other similar sources of information. The purpose of the addiction is to block whatever goes on inside addicts that they fear they cannot handle. This includes a whole range of feelings such as rage, anger, fear, and anxiety as well as pleasurable feelings like joy, excitement, or creativity. Their frozen feelings also keep addicts from differentiating between feelings and from knowing the fine nuances that make fear different from anxiety, or joy different from excitement.

Unfortunately, in the addictive system, our feelings are often seen as weaknesses. The perfectly adjusted man or woman is the one who appears to be "above" his or her feelings. Our addictions block our feelings. Instead of dealing with the feeling and learning from it, we get busy getting a drink or a snack when we feel anxiety. We have heard it said, "When the going gets tough, the tough go shopping." The tough distract themselves by becoming consumers so as not to feel that things are "tough." The inability to feel is a serious issue in the addictive system. As we are more and more removed from our feelings and awareness, we are removed from information about who we are and what we really believe. We become malleable and out of touch with our own ethics. We eventually lose our very lives.

Ethical deterioration is the inevitable outcome of immersion in the addictive system. It is easy to understand how this happens. If your life is taken up by lying to yourself and others, attempting to control, perfectionism, denial, grabbing what you can for yourself, and refusing to let in information that would alter the addictive paradigm, then you are *spiritually bankrupt.*

It is interesting to note that AA has always maintained that alcoholism is first and foremost a spiritual disease. The addictive process attacks one's morality and deep spiritual values. It is easy to see how addicts have lost their personal morality: they would cheat, steal, and lie to get their fix. Perhaps it is not so clear with the system.

We believe the addictive system invites us to compromise our personal morality by inviting us to engage in all the processes just described. Besides establishing a social norm in which it is acceptable to cheat, steal, and lie, the very use of addictions separates us from our spiritual awareness. To the extent that religious systems are caught in the same processes as the addict, they themselves support our remaining in the addictive system. Indeed, whenever we confuse religion with spirituality, we are opting for the structure, control, and rules of an addictive system. This reliance on religion may remove us from the inner search only we can do from the depths of our own being.

This is merely a cursory treatment of some of the major characteristics of an addict and the addictive system. Further descriptions can be found in the literature. Schaef, herself, details many others, including *crisis orientation, depression, stress, abnormal thinking processes, forgetfulness, dependency, negativism, defensiveness, projection, tunnel vision,* and *fear.* [2] People who work with addicts know these patterns well. We are only now seeing how they function at a systems level and on a global level.

PROCESS

In addition to these characteristics, the addictive system has certain underlying processes that become extremely powerful when left unnamed. Process is the underlying, true meaning of a communication or the feeling in a communication. The process of a message is frequently even more powerful than the content of the message and is what people will usually respond to when the two differ. For example, in a sales meeting, the sales manager *says* to his reps that even though this has been a poor month, he knows the reps will do better next month. His tone of voice is cynical and judgmental; his teeth are clenched, his eyes narrow, and his neck strained. Everyone leaves the meeting with the process meaning: the *message* is he is furious.

Processes are difficult to name and to change. We have looked at some of the content of the addictive system; now we must describe some of the processes. As Schaef says, the processes of the addictive system are its secret strengths; they are what perpetuate it; they have essentially gone unnamed.

There are six processes of the addictive system we want to consider: the promise, the pseudopodic ego, the external reference, invalidation, fabricating personality conflicts, and dualism.

THE PROCESS OF THE PROMISE

The process of the promise takes us out of our present, asks us to devalue our experience and focus upon expectations. The promise directs us eagerly to the future, to some hoped-for reward, while keeping us out of touch with the present. It encourages us to live out our lives on expectations. The sociologist Marie Augusta Neal has written extensively on the promise of the church to people of various economic classes. The poor hear sermons that say, "We suffer and are deprived in this life in order to have a reward in heaven." The rich hear sermons that say, "Our riches in this life are the sign of God's love for us now." Neither group is prompted to look at the present reality.

The addict's loved ones always trust in the hope that things are going to get better—the alcoholic will stop drinking, or the family will get out of debt. In an organization, it is a certain group of employees that will make a drastic turnaround. Unfortunately, this constant focus on the future is the very thing that keeps everyone mired in the present, and therefore in the problem. The "promise" is itself a fix that gives temporary relief from the here and now.

THE PROCESS OF THE PSEUDOPODIC EGO

The pseudopodic ego is a process the addictive system uses to absorb and utilize for itself everything that is different from itself. It is a type of colonization. In this process, things that represent a different system become absorbed into the addictive system. For example, in an organization with which we consulted women within the company had made several critiques of company procedures. Overall the management practices at this company were terrible, and the public image of the company in the community was not good. Management acceded to the women's requests in one part of the system, then used that one change to brag about how responsive they were to employees, and especially how well they were doing. In actuality, nothing significant changed in the company, and scores of women eventually left. In essence, they used the women's suggestions to perpetuate the existing policies. The pseudopodic ego of the addictive system is this kind of process. It absorbs and incorporates differences into itself, owns these differences, and then uses them to perpetuate the system intact. One must carefully check to see if the status quo is maintained when an illusion of openness and flexibility is projected.

THE PROCESS OF EXTERNAL REFERENCING

The external referencing process is basic to the kind of self-definition one finds in the addictive system. We develop our sense of self by the process of focusing outside ourselves. We learn who we are and what we value by reliance on outside authorities, on families, schools, churches, and other institutions.

In an addictive system, we tend to judge our success by how other people perceive us. We become adept at learning what pleases others, and we get busy doing those things. In the process of the addictive system, our point of reference is always outside ourselves. We become progressively less capable of feeling what we feel or want, and we do not even consider seeking validation inside the self. In the addictive system, this process is related to the self-centeredness of the addict, who has no boundaries and no way of distinguishing between the self and the other. When one has no boundaries, the self and the other become indistinguishable and any sense of self or true recognition of the existence of the other is lost.

THE PROCESS OF INVALIDATION

Invalidation is the process the addictive system uses to define into nonexistence those ideas and experiences that the system cannot know, understand, or most importantly, control. Invalidation is one of the main hallmarks of a closed system. It acknowledges that divergent ideas exist but will not let them into the frame of reference of the system, *and* it refuses even to recognize the existence of processes that are threatening to it.

As we have said earlier, one of the biggest problems with addictions is that they numb us to our feelings and take us out of touch with our experiences. Because we are less adept at recognizing processes, they are largely unavailable to us and to others.

We referred earlier to the scientific method and worldview as a system some believe is entropic and no longer viable. One of its problems is that it narrowly defines what is worth knowing and what is not worth knowing. Much of what is not worth knowing comes from the imagination, intuition, spirituality, and other realms of consciousness and experience. At its extreme, the scientific worldview said, If it cannot be measured and controlled, it is not real. It is easy to see how the scientific method belief system and the addictive system espouse and support the same process of invalidation. This process truncates information and knowledge.

THE PROCESS OF FABRICATING PERSONALITY CONFLICTS

The fabricating personality conflicts process of the addictive system is similar to the process of invalidating. The personality conflict process attempts to dismiss or discount inputs to particular individuals or groups by generating the illusion that personalities are in conflict. This technique serves to discount the bearer of unwanted information. In the addictive system, the process of fabricating a personality conflict is usually a way of not dealing with a truth that would threaten the denial system. In open systems, much information can be taken in, considered, utilized, and set aside without being a threat to the identity of the group or system. In the addictive system, accurate information is always a threat to the status quo. The illusion of a personality conflict sets up a diversion that moves the focus away from the real issue, which is frequently the confrontation of some addiction or addictive functioning.

THE PROCESS OF DUALISM

Lastly, we come to the process of dualism. Dualism undergirds almost all the characteristics of the addictive system. In fact, most of the characteristics of the addictive system emerge from dualistic thinking.

The process of dualistic thinking has several functions in the addictive system. First, it allows us to simplify a very complex world into two choices, with the underlying assumption that if we can decide which end of the dualism is right, we will be right and justified. One can see that this kind of thinking is closely related to the illusion of control. Dualism allows us to relegate a very complex and ambiguous universe to two simplistic choices. Dualisms create a false sense of stability in assuming that all movement must be between the two given alternatives. Some people just do not feel that they can cope with unlimited options.

It often happens, in dualistic thinking, that neither option is acceptable, yet the rigidity of the dualism prevents people from generating options. In the addictive system, the continual moving back and forth between two choices serves to keep one stuck. Inevitably, neither of the two choices in a dualism looks desirable. The "stuck place" of this dualistic thinking also keeps one constantly externally referenced. The way out of a dualism is to make a choice that is consistent with one's inner process, one's spirituality, or being. As long as we are kept busy with the dualism, we do not make the inner journey to clarity.

CO-DEPENDENCE

No discussion of addictive functioning would be complete without looking at the role of the co-dependent. As we said earlier, historically a co-dependent was thought to be a person who is in a love or marriage relationship with an alcoholic or other addict. Later developments in the addiction field have described co-dependence as a constellation of behaviors that emerge in relation to the addictive system and dysfunctional family patterns.

In terms of our system concern, it is imperative to recognize that the co-dependent and the addict are simultaneously different and the same. One calls forth and supports the other. If people quit playing the co-dependent role, addictions could not survive, for addicts must have the collusion of co-dependents to maintain their closed addictive system. Similarly, when addicts are recovering they can barely tolerate being around co-dependents and know that the disease of co-dependency threatens their recovery. They are two sides of the same coin.

Co-dependents exhibit some of the same characteristics as addicts, but in a different form. Let us explore lying, for example. An addict will tell a bald-faced lie to prevent his or her supply from being threatened. "Were you drinking?" "No," says the addict, looking you straight in the eye and reeking of liquor. The co-dependent's dishonesty tends toward doing and saying the "nice thing" rather than saying what he or she really feels. If you are a co-dependent and you are allergic to smoke, when your co-worker asks if you mind if he or she smokes, you say no. You do not want to hurt the other person's feelings. It would not be nice. This is an example of co-dependence.

Co-dependents frequently spend much of their time taking care of others. Many enter professions that allow them to continue caring for others: nursing, counseling, social work, the ministry, medicine, psychology. Those who work with co-dependents report that they have low self-esteem and will literally kill themselves to be liked by others. One of the most prevalent addictions of co-dependents is workaholism.

Co-dependents are servers, volunteers, and the ones who set aside their own needs to serve the needs of others. They end up exhausted and burned out and rewarded by the system for their thoughtfulness and giving. The problem is that co-dependents are so giving that they end up giving away themselves. Co-dependents become hollow, out of touch with their own processes, and depressed.

Co-dependents are sufferers. They are selfless to the point of illness. The society's concept of the "good Christian martyr" is the perfect co-dependent. Co-dependents complain a lot, but when you offer to help, they refuse your help—not wanting to burden you and preferring, in their illusion of control and self-centeredness, to do it themselves. Co-dependents carry an identifiable constellation of diseases. They tend toward ulcers, high blood pressure, colitis, back pain, and certain types of cancer. It is believed that, like the disease of addiction, co-dependence is a fatal disease. In fact, there is some evidence that co-dependents who are in addictive relationships tend to die younger than addicts do.

Co-dependents are frequently in relations with addicts and other co-dependents. Though frequently not a drug or alcohol addict themselves, they do use other substances or processes compulsively, such as coffee, nicotine, food, or work. Their disease is more subtle and serious, harder to detect and more socially acceptable than that of the active addict. The culture views alcohol and drug addiction negatively, whereas the behaviors of the co-dependent are actually fostered. No wonder it is so hard to recover from co-dependence! In fact, many professionals in the treatment field claim that co-dependence is far more difficult to treat than other addictions. They also contend that the helping professions have themselves become the practice of the disease of co-dependence.

Co-dependents are experts in external referencing and impression management. They spend most of their time understanding the needs of others and picking up subtle cues about what others want from them. At the same time they are astute observers. They intuitively know what responses are required in most situations, and they can give them. Their impression management disguises a wide-ranging dishonesty that is experienced by others as niceness, righteousness, and an unlimited capacity for understanding and listening. Co-dependents will rarely come right out and tell you what they want. They are experts at vagueness, manipulation, rumor, and gossip. Eventually, they usually get their way, and rarely do they have to take any direct responsibility for getting what they want. Culturally, the co-dependent looks like the loving, giving person, yet as we work with co-dependents we find that underneath their composed exterior, they are frequently angry, depressed, and extremely controlling and manipulative.

Obviously, the disease of co-dependence plays an essential part in keeping the addictive system going, and in a very real way, it is inextricably bound with the addictive system: there would be no addictive system without it. In this way, addictions and co-dependence are two aspects of the same system.

Now that we have clarified our terms, we move on to describe the four major ways in which addictions function in organizations. None of these categories is discrete; that is to say, there is definite overlap between and among them. Yet, each of the four has unique dynamics, and we feel that it is necessary to understand all four, how they function and how they interrelate if one is to begin the process of evolving healthy, life-enhancing organizations.

III

THE FOUR MAJOR FORMS OF ADDICTION IN ORGANIZATIONS

1. Organizations in Which a Key Person Is an Addict

In the course of our consulting, we have worked with several organizations where we saw that recognizing that a significant person in the organization was an active addict was the *key* to understanding what was going on in the organization itself.

In Section I we referred to a book, *The Neurotic Organization,* that describes the unhealthy climate created by top executives. *The Neurotic Organization* asserts that companies do tend to take on the personalities of key executives. We extend this analysis further. We believe it is not just the top executives whose basic character sets the tone of the organization, it is any person who is "key" in the system in either line or staff. In fact, in addictive organizations, an active addict can have tremendous influence, because an addict's behavior draws an excessive amount of attention and is a constant drain on the time and energy of others.

How does this happen, and why? First of all, the addictive process is a very powerful disease process. It is a "cunning, powerful, baffling, and patient" disease. In addition, those who are actively operating in this disease become so confused and confusing to others that they begin to isolate themselves and cease to be subject to the normal feedback mechanisms that other employees face. The higher the person is in the company, the less likely he or she will be closely scrutinized, and the more the disease progresses, the more isolated the addict becomes.

In a small mid-western manufacturing company with which we consulted, a comptroller who was an active alcoholic suffered a series of blackouts. During these blackouts he authorized the purchase of forty new automobiles for salespeople. Of course, the car dealers in the town loved this man, and the sales staff was incredulous but believed that top management must know what they were doing. Up until the time of this incident, which cost the company over $300,000, this man had been described as "eccentric" and/or as having "a strange personality." No one saw him for what he was, a "drunk" on a rampage. For this company, an alcoholic was someone falling down drunk in the street. This man was seen as somewhat peculiar, but doing his job. The most anyone proposed was that the comptroller could use some psychological help and that he needed to be supervised more closely.

Both of these solutions are responses typical of organizations. Rather than see the problem as the addictive process, they define it psychologically and treat it with psychological intervention. The other strategy companies use is to exert some kind of control over the addict, thereby frequently exacerbating the problems, because focusing on control puts the company into the same addictive system as the addict, that is, a system operating out of the illusion of control.

The reaction of the company was to look for every kind of traditional solution, which is typical of the naïveté or functional blindness of those in the addictive organization. Most people in the addictive organization have been trained to act and think addictively, and one of the chief characteristics of addiction is denial. Even though crises push us to re-form our old concepts and abandon them, the main line of defense is first to refuse to see what is happening, and then to fall back on an older, familiar style. Blake and Mouton first documented this tendency when they observed that under stress people go to a familiar "backup" style that has been deeply integrated into their personalities. They do this even after they have been trained in more humanistic and more effective styles of management.

The company in our example tried all the usual backup solutions: suggesting psychological help, providing closer supervision, and sending the comptroller to workshops on communication and management training. When the situation reached a crisis that was about to endanger the rest of the company as well as the comptroller, they knew that they needed further help and sought outside consultation. The company was about to hit a financial bottom just as the comptroller was about to hit a personal bottom. Fortunately, in this particular company, the employee was sent for treatment for chemical dependency and returned to his job, where he is continuing to deal with the effects of the "auto caper." He also openly shares with management and employees what he has learned about the addictive disease and has activated a recovery for the entire organization.

The other focus of *The Neurotic Organization* is the identification of executive leadership styles. The styles described are the dramatic, the depressive, the paranoid, the compulsive, and the schizoid. The authors believe these styles are dysfunctional for the executives they studied, although they feel that a combination of styles might be more workable.

As we studied these styles, it occurred to us that Kets deVries and Miller had gathered valuable data and then made a wrong interpretation. We believe this happens when the researchers, for whatever reason, do not have or ignore an important piece of the puzzle. All of the "neurotic behaviors" they describe are found in the addictive personality. For example, they describe the compulsive type as characterized by perfectionism, insistence that others submit to their way of doing things, dogmatism, and obstinacy. We have already identified the addict as compulsive, perfectionistic, and controlling. They describe the paranoid type as cold, rational, and unemotional. This coincides with the frozen feelings of the addict, and the defense mechanism of projection is dominant in both the paranoid and the addict. The dramatic type was given to self-dramatization and incessant drawing of attention to self. This type fits with what we have named the self-centeredness of the addict, which is always accompanied by mood swings and a crisis orientation. The depressive, who harbors feelings of guilt and inadequacy and a diminished ability to think clearly, fits what we described as key characteristics of the co-dependent and the addict. The schizoid, who is detached, not involved, estranged, with lack of interest in present or future, is what we saw as exhibiting ethical deterioration and out-of-touch feelings, frequently using chemicals or process addictions to maintain detachment and distance from the present.

The entire constellation of behaviors of the "neurotic executive" are the characteristics of the active addict, the addictive system, and the co-dependent. Interestingly, *The Neurotic Organization* claims that healthy functioning will result if executives find a better neurotic style than their present style. They counsel a combination of styles.

We would say that such a proposal is tantamount to telling an alcoholic to stop drinking so much and start taking some cocaine in addition. The real problem has never been addressed. The behaviors the authors describe are all behaviors of an active addict and an addictive system. You cannot trade one addictive behavior for another and hope the organization will move to more healthy ways of functioning.

The therapeutic community at large has denied the role of addictions in dysfunction. When addiction is the "norm" for the society or when persons are addicts or come from addictive families, unless they are recovering, their denial systems tend to remain intact and they just do not "see" what is going on at a systemic level. In fact, sometimes seeing the pieces themselves serves to "protect the addictive supply" and draw attention away from the larger systemic problem. In this way, the addictive process is supported and can continue.

The power of key people in organizations is related to their influence and to the networks they have built. When they are nonrecovering addicts, one power they have is the power to bring a company to the brink of destruction.

We were contacted recently by an internal consultant from a very large Fortune 500 corporation. This man believed that they had an incipient tragedy developing in the company. He said he was concerned about a vice-president who was responsible for a division that accounted for 25 percent of the profit of the entire corporation. The vice-president was exhibiting all the behaviors of an active addict. He had become increasingly controlling and perfectionistic; he was having memory loss; and his behavior was self-centered and dishonest.

The internal consultant, who himself was a recovering co-dependent, recognized these behaviors as addictive and knew the disease was progressive. He had no hope the vice-president would get help for himself, by himself. The consultant's concern was for the man and for the company. "I'm afraid this guy is going to wipe out, but he'll take the division down with him before he goes," said the internal consultant. "It would be absolutely disastrous for the company."

Compounding the seriousness of this situation was that the vice-president had developed a very sophisticated "con" (which is typical for an active addict), so that most of his behaviors were excused. In fact, many of his irrational behaviors were overlooked by his staff precisely because he was the boss. We do believe that frequently those in high-power positions have a wider range of dysfunction allowed to them than those with less power in the organization. In true alcoholic fashion, he began to isolate himself, so that even those close to him had difficulty getting the information that would have clearly indicated a pattern of personal and organizational destructiveness. His company has yet to do an intervention, and his division is on the brink of disaster.

It is important to recognize that it was both the vice-president's cunning and baffling behavior and the organization's deliberate blindness to a pattern of trouble that created this situation. If either party in this addictive system had stepped out of the disease process, the entire addictive system would have crumbled. In this case, the addict was safe as long as the co-dependents maintained their denial. Basically, the co-dependents remained oblivious or covered up his behavior, while the addict became sicker with a progressive and fatal disease and was not given the help he needed.

High-tech companies, with their stress and competitiveness, are not the only ones to face this disease. Even those whose work is the treatment of addictions find themselves mired in the very thing they are supposed to be experts in detecting. A good example is a psychiatric treatment center in a major metropolitan hospital complex with which we consulted several years ago.

Initially, we had been contacted to do an organizational assessment and to work with the treatment staff of this center. The center had been open for about three years, and it was experiencing increasing problems with organizational structure and personnel. In the course of our assessment interviews, it became apparent that a key team member was a nonrecovering "dry alcoholic." This person (Sue) had been to treatment for alcoholism and was no longer using chemicals, but she was not actively involved in a program of recovery and was not making a personal system shift. She was operating like an active drunk even though she was not drinking, which is the definition of a "dry drunk" or "dry alcoholic." How did we know this woman was on a dry drunk? Here are some of the behaviors we encountered. First of all, she was deeply dishonest. She was employed at the treatment center full time and simultaneously was holding down two other full-time jobs in other places in the city. We discovered this when we uncovered the fact that nobody, including the administrator, knew what she did with her time or where she was most of the time. Upon interviewing the patients, we found that she rarely kept her appointments and commitments to them and was rarely around.

During a series of interviews with the other staff, they kept saying things about the center's administrator of a highly personal nature. When we probed further, asking how people knew these things, they said they did not have the information from their own experience but that Sue had said they should mention it to us. Sue was involved in a second level of dishonesty. She refused to speak to us directly about her concerns with the administrator. Instead, she funneled the information through others, who did not even share her concern. Clearly, she did not want to be linked with the information she was spreading around, because much of it was geared at questioning the integrity of the administrator.

Gossip and rumor abounded in the organization. As we tracked down the source of the rumors, they all led back to one person, Sue. This process kept the staff in continual upheaval, for they were constantly trying to deal with a myriad of rumors. They engaged in endless one-on-one meetings in which they tried to clear up what was going on. Since much of their free time was occupied with rumor management, they had little time to focus on professional issues related to treatment. In addition, there was no attention to or energy left for focusing on Sue and seeing her behavior for what it was: addictive. She created confusion in the system, and the confusion left people powerless to do anything other than deal with the confusion. They also, like good co-dependents, chose to remain ignorant of what was really happening.

Lastly, Sue used a very interesting—and common—addictive process to avoid being confronted. It soon became apparent that the consultants were aware of the addictive functioning in the center, and specifically concerned about Sue, her disease, and its effect upon the center. Very early in the process, Sue let it be known that she had a "personality conflict" with the consultants. We found this very interesting, because we had had very little interaction with her and, in fact, had spent most of our time listening and interviewing. It may be that only addicts possess the ability to have an instant and thorough personality conflict based on little or no interaction with a person! The purpose of the fabricated personality conflict was to discredit the perception of the consultants and, by doing so, make our assessment of what was going on in the organization questionable.

When we confronted the fabricated personality conflict along with the other behaviors we observed, Sue announced that it was "her or us" (dramatic!) and offered her resignation on the spot if we were not terminated as consultants. Luckily for the center and the administrator, who had been looking for a way to let her go for months, Sue was taken at her word; her resignation was promptly accepted.

Sue's behavior raises another typical technique addicts tend to use. It is the process of setting up a me(us)—you(they) situation in which people believe they have to take sides. This is a form of the dualistic process we mentioned earlier. When Sue set it up as either her or us, she set up a dualistic situation in which the practicing co-dependents in the organization immediately felt they had to take sides, and it was easy to see the panic in their faces. Sue was clearly acting out of her disease in setting up an impossible situation, yet the consultants were outsiders, and the loyalty of the staff was to Sue. What were they to do?

Luckily for us, we immediately recognized the "side-taking" dualism that was being set up, knew that it was a ploy of the addictive process, and refused to play. As consultants, we brought the focus back to the needs of the organization and Sue. We used this opportunity to recommend relapse treatment for Sue, with her continuation in the organization being contingent upon her going for treatment. She chose not to go; the administrator accepted her resignation; and we moved on to the needs of the center and the staff. As consultants we had exhibited concern for the organization *and* concern for Sue. We believe that if we had not been aware of this process of the addictive disease, we could have been sucked into the addictive process and become enmeshed in it.

In this case an employee chose to leave rather than get better. It is also a case in which one can see the tremendous power of the addict when she elects to involve other people in her addictive behavior. The rest of the staff had been keeping secrets, carrying tales, and protecting Sue from experiencing the consequences of her behavior. They were acting like good nonrecovering organizational co-dependents.

Look at the insidiousness of the process of this disease. The very people whose daily work was providing treatment and facilitating recovery were as deeply mired in disease as those who came to them for treatment. Their knowledge and skill could not help them if they were willing to enter the disease process with Sue. Compare the secretiveness surrounding addictions with the attitude we have toward another disease, say cancer. We are much more open to discussing someone with heart disease, getting information on the person's progress, asking whether there is something to be done, and gradually supporting the treatment. We do not make the person or the disease invisible. With addictions we are much less ready to intervene, to be open, and to confront the problem. This reticence, we believe, is due to the addictive system itself, which uses denial as the main defense against seeing and acknowledging what is happening. As long as something is hidden, it is powerful.

From the example of the treatment center and many others we have encountered, we are convinced that no one is immune to these addictive behaviors, regardless of their life-style or training. In two of the aforementioned situations, there was enough openness in the system that key people were eventually recognized as addicts and their power to completely undermine the company minimized. In groups that are more closed, or that have extremely hierarchical or authoritarian leadership structures, leaders are less assailable. Consequently, their disease can have more disastrous effects on the group.

A severe case we encountered as consultants took place ten years ago in one of the most unlikely of places—a monastery in southern Germany. Because of the authority structure of the monastery, which is supported by a centuries-old theology, the head monk, the abbot, has complete responsibility for the monks of the abbey, from the oldest to the youngest. The abbot has a council that assists him in decision making, but in the practical running of the monastery, the abbot is the ultimate authority.

In this particular situation, a team of consultants had preceded us. They had attempted organizational-structural change and found themselves blocked at every turn. They admitted to feeling overwhelmed and desperate at what they called "addictive behaviors," and they recommended that we come in.

We found a system in complete disarray. First, the abbot himself was an active alcoholic, a closet drinker. In addition, there were several other men in the monastery who were active addicts. We uncovered drug, alcohol, and sex addiction, plus scores of others who needed physical and psychological help.

We were frequently met at the door of the monastery with, as we came to call them, "tales of fresh disaster." A brother had been sent away because he abused a student; several monks were suffering deep depression and physical illness. All these crises were related calmly, with almost no affect. Everyone knew about them, and they were told to us as if from a fog.

Because this system was so closed and there was such an abundance of sick behavior, the individuals in the group had come to see this behavior as the norm in the group; it was expected. They did not like it; they were upset by it; and they expected it. Ethical deterioration was rampant, accompanied by depression and much physical illness. Some men shook their heads as they spoke, and indicated how powerless they felt to change either their own behavior or that of others.

The abbot's alcoholism caused a kind of dysfunctioning in the monastery similar to that of most addicts as they function in organizations and in their personal lives. For example, alcoholics and addicts typically make poor financial judgments. Frequently, it is more important for them to be liked than to have sound fiscal policies, as we saw in the earlier example of the comptroller who purchased forty cars. He was certainly well liked all over town. In this case, the monastery was running a business for its financial support, but the business was on the verge of bankruptcy. Rather than do the unpopular thing and close the business, the abbot kept it going with money from the monastery. By the time we arrived, they were in danger of losing all their assets. Very few people knew this, however, because the books were open only to a few.

The situation was similar to what one sees in the addictive family system. Indeed, since the abbot was the "spiritual father" of the monks, most of them related to him from that perspective. In addition to familial roles, we observed three other modalities among these men, all typical of the addictive system. In relation to the alcoholic abbot, there was (1) blind following—nothing was wrong with him, nothing was wrong with the business—(2) a confused scurrying around trying to find out what was going on by speaking to each other but no direct confrontation of the abbot, and (3) acting out. In the pattern often seen in the alcoholic family, various members took on various alcoholic family roles. Some became hero children, who looked after others and tried to be good and keep the monastery going. Others were scapegoats. They were troublemakers, who drew attention to themselves and away from the abbot. Some were lost children, isolating from the trouble, creating worlds of their own, and feeling that they could never be included in what was happening in the monastery. Some of the lost children moved away from the monastery, putting physical distance between them and the group. Finally, there were the mascots, those who were the clowns and jokesters, who kept things light, socialized a lot, and felt that things would improve if only people did not take themselves too seriously and prayed a lot. They took attention away from the problems and helped people temporarily feel good.

In a system as authoritarian and closed as this, there was little likelihood that the group itself would do an intervention with the abbot. Of course this was exacerbated by the fact that too many group members were active alcoholics themselves. Because of the self-centeredness of their own disease, they could not see beyond themselves. Others were thoroughly involved in their co-dependence. Essentially the entire system functioned as an active addictive system. In these systems, outside intervention is the usual route to change and awareness. This did occur, first through the work of the consultants, and eventually, through intervention by the church hierarchy. The acting abbot has taken complete control; property has been sold, their business closed, and there are grave questions about whether the abbey will continue to exist.

Whenever people are granted a huge degree of power, they can affect "followers" greatly. We consulted with a church whose minister was suffering from sexual addiction. Several members of the church felt uneasy about the sexual innuendos he made, which they felt were inappropriate, and others were uncomfortable around him, feeling that his behavior was sometimes "sexualized" and embarrassing to them.

Because the church itself frequently functions as an addictive organization, especially in the way it handles issues like sexuality, it often attracts men like this minister. The structure of the system within which he was operating was involved in a dualism about sexuality. The dualism is, on the one hand, repression of sex and things sexual and, on the other, obsession with sex. In other words, because the church itself was so repressive about matters of sexuality, there was an inordinate amount of interest in and concern about sexuality. You can see that as long as one stays stuck in the dualism, sex remains a chief focus, for one is constantly swinging between the shame and "no never" of repression and the intrigue of obsession. Whenever the minister tried to repress his addiction, his behavior quickly swung to the other end of the dualism, and he found himself slipping in off-color jokes and acting out sexually.

Although many parishioners were uncomfortable around him and with his behavior, they insisted on protecting him. They protected him for a number of reasons, all related to their own co-dependence. Being good co-dependents, the parishioners preferred to ignore their own perception of what was going on. They feared sharing what they were feeling and seeing thereby risking that someone else would feel uncomfortable. Good co-dependents hate unpleasantness of any kind, and they especially avoid "making someone else feel bad." (Note the self-centeredness of this attitude, as if the co-dependent has the power to "make" others feel a certain way.)

The minister's role removed him from the usual scrutinizing we tend to give other people. At some level he was expected to be "above all that" and not human; also, the nature of the minister's work was such that he was isolated to a certain degree. He worked alone and rarely participated in ongoing groups where his behavior could be observed closely over time.

Meanwhile, the minister is suffering. He leads a secret life and has many fears that keep him from functioning well in the church. The parish suffers because they cannot get the kind of service in ministry they want and need. In the end, everyone keeps the secret and denies what is really going on. In the end, everyone loses.

In the addictive organization, everyone loses. This is because the addictive disease is a "contagious" disease that is insidious, progressive, and fatal. Individuals have their disease, and by reason of the relationship, we experience our disease when we get involved with another. From the examples given, it should be clear that even attempts not to get involved with people who are operating out of their disease is a way of participating in the disease, because when we deny or ignore what is going on, we become part of the disease.

From the perspective of traditional organizational dynamics, our example of the key person in the addictive organization would be seen differently, we suspect. Many of these cases could be defined as issues of change, participation, leadership, management incompetency, or personality conflicts. However, given the knowledge of the addictive system, the way it functions and the impact of individual addicts, we begin to have a different perspective on these issues.

We begin to appreciate the holographic notion of the problem and to understand why certain solutions have not always worked in the past. Sometimes key leaders who exhibit some of the characteristics we outlined here are removed. Our experience has shown that the removal helped initially; there was relief at first. Then we became aware that the group was not much different, even with the manager gone. That was because though the addict was gone, the co-dependents remained, and they continued in their system practicing their disease.

The lesson we took from these experiences is that all parts of the system must be treated if a real and thorough change is to take place. Leaders and key people have great influence, and this influence is multiplied as the system itself becomes increasingly addictive. To get treatment for the individual addict in an organization is important. It is progress and results in important change. Yet one must also treat the whole system. Treating a whole system leads to change at all levels of the organization, which is necessary if a change is to be effective.

We believe it is clear that when a key person in an organization functions as an addict the organization is profoundly affected. We will now show how others, as well as the addict, repeat dysfunctional personal and family patterns and cause organizations to develop an addictive way of functioning.

2. Taking Your Disease with You into the Organization, or the Reality of Replication

A person not involved in active recovery is probably part of the problem. In this section, we will address all the ways the addict, the adult child of the alcoholic, and the co-dependent repeat behaviors in organizations that they have learned in their families and other addictive settings. But first we take a brief look at some terms and some statistics.

DEFINITIONS

As we mentioned earlier, an addict is a person who is powerless over a substance or a process in his or her life to the point that progressive immersion in the addiction will lead to death. All addictions are fatal, although addictions are also the only disease for which recovery is guaranteed if the person addicted begins a program of recovery.

No one knows exactly how many active addicts there are in the United States. The estimates on the known number of recovering alcoholics alone is also unclear and essentially a guess, since the AA program is anonymous, and we do not have accurate statistics. Remember that any statistics we do have relate only to alcoholics; there are no real statistics for drug, food, sex, work, or relationship addicts.

An adult child of an alcoholic (ACOA or ACA) is a person who grew up in a family in which one or more parents was an alcoholic, or in a family that repeats alcoholic or addictive patterns. Adult children may not be addicts themselves as adults, although they can be. However, ACOAs carry a unique set of emotional problems and specific personality disorders that affect their lives. Identification of the personality characteristics is relatively recent, and the first national organization of adult children of alcoholics (National Association of Children of Alcoholics) is only a few years old.

Statistics vary on the number of ACOAs in the United States. Robert Goldberg puts the number at 28–34 million, or 15 percent of the U.S. population. We believe that this estimate is extremely low.

The designation of co-dependent is wider than that of addict or ACOA. According to descriptions we cited earlier, Wegscheider-Cruse and others believe a co-dependent is anyone who had an alcoholic parent or grandparent, is in a marriage or love relationship with an alcoholic or other addict, or who came from an emotionally repressive family. Estimates on the number of co-dependents in the United States range up to 96 percent of the population.

From these definitions, it can be presumed that every ACOA is by definition also a co-dependent. Every co-dependent is not necessarily an adult child of alcoholics. Addicts can be ACOAs and co-dependents, although they may not be (though most addicts are thought to have the disease of co-dependence underlying their addiction). Many addicts find that they begin their recovery from their primary addiction only to find they must then face their co-dependence and start that recovery process also. What is obvious is that the addictive process is handed down through families, so people growing up in alcoholic or otherwise addictive families do not escape unscathed but take the characteristics with them into all other relationships and facets of their lives. This then leads to a particular worldview, which becomes an illusionary reality. Writers in the field cite enormous statistics for the number of people with addictive disease and this is why. It is the reason also why a writer like Schaef can state unequivocally that addictions are now the norm for the society. These people are not an isolated problem off on the side somewhere that does not reflect the society at large. They are the norm.

Much attention has been focused on the dynamics of the addictive process in families and in individuals. Very little attention has been paid to how the addict, the ACOA, and the co-dependent replicate the patterns they develop in their families and their personal lives in the workplace.

ALCOHOLICS AT WORK

We know, for example, that alcoholics can and often do repeat at work some of the same behaviors they exhibit at home—they lie, they intimidate, they make poor judgments, and they are forgetful. As we saw in the previous section, they are frequently the focus of attention at work, and their ability to engender chaos in a situation is awesome indeed.

ADULT CHILDREN OF ALCOHOLICS AT WORK

Adult children of alcoholics have special difficulties in the workplace. Robert N. Goldberg describes the issues almost all ACOAs must face at some point in their career.[1] We have borrowed his categories; the examples are our own.

PERFECTIONISM/SELF-CRITICISM

As Goldberg states, ACOAs feel they must do each job perfectly. They berate themselves for even the smallest mistakes. Their self-criticism is so extreme that they disregard praise, feeling it could not possibly be true. They tend to put in inordinate amounts of overtime, in order to ensure that projects are just right. In the years before memory typewriters, we knew secretaries who would type and retype an entire page if they made one mistake, never using correction fluid. We also know a law professor who insists that essay answers on student exams be exactly one thousand words long, no more, no less. You can imagine how much time the students spend focusing on the content of the questions! This is the replication of the disease in the workplace.

WORKAHOLISM

The addiction of choice for many ACOAs is overwork. Some do it to make up for feelings of insecurity or inferiority, thereby constantly going the extra mile. Others are unable to say no to the demands of co-workers and bosses. Goldberg hypothesizes that many ACOAs are workaholics because they prefer to stick with what they know best, and ACOAs are better at work than they are at personal relationships, which they find difficult and anxiety producing. ACOAs may very well be the most dedicated workers in the company. They are rarely laggards. Most organizations love their dedication and productivity. However, while they are excelling at work, they tend to be dying emotionally.

RIGIDITY IN THINKING

ACOAs lack flexibility; their thinking tends to be dualistic. They think in terms of black and white, and right and wrong. Their rigidity, combined with their perfectionism, leads to their belief that there is one and only one correct solution for everything. They are rarely open to options. They can be maddening to work with because they will frequently give verbal assent to something and then go ahead with their own plans. Their motto is "I'll do it my way." A vice-president of a savings and loan confided to us that he would spend hours in conference with his immediate supervisor and then go through contortions trying to figure out how he could do it "his way" while still appearing to honor the commitments he had made to the branch manager. He was practicing his disease at work.

CRISIS HANDLING

ACOAs tend to be superb during a crisis. In fact, they are coolest when things are falling apart. This is probably because they spent their childhood in addictive families that were fraught with unpredictability, where crisis was usual. They never knew whether they would meet violence, tenderness, or complete rejection from the intoxicated parent. They learned to be calm under the most extreme conditions. Obviously, if their households were violent, their ability to stay calm may have saved their lives.

The ability to stay calm during crisis is an admirable quality in the workplace. Unfortunately, the crisis orientation becomes a way of life for ACOAs. They have trouble with calm. A manufacturing executive confided to us that he felt lifeless during periods of calm in the company, and occasionally he was aware he fabricated conflicts and fueled crisis in order to produce excitement. Since many ACOAs have "frozen" their feelings, it takes extreme conditions to provoke them to feel at all; consequently, they often intentionally create a "big bang." Since they are not attuned to the finer nuances of feelings that are available to people during periods of calm, the only feelings they feel are the intense ones.

TEAMWORK

In this age of entrepreneurial teams in corporations, the ACOAs have difficulty adjusting. Generally, they would rather be left alone; they are not team players. Many ACOAs never learn the rudimentary lessons of cooperation in the family unit. The family rarely operated as a unit, and children grew up isolated and alone. In fact, participation in the family was a source of pain and fear. Being alone was safe. Consequently, many ACOAs come to the workplace with very poor skills and little or no experience in working together.

Goldberg identifies three major reasons why ACOAs are poor team members: (1) they have difficulty listening and communicating; (2) they have difficulty giving and receiving criticism; and (3) they have a strong need for control.[2] The rigidity and perfectionism referred to earlier, along with high need for control, produces a take-charge personality that either wants to run the show or opt out altogether.

We have also found that ACOAs can be very unpredictable on teams. Sometimes they are overresponsible, carrying the majority of the load of the team, and at other times they drop all responsibility completely. The close working relationship of teams seems to tap into all their unresolved family issues, creating anxiety and frequently causing extreme behavior swings.

As supervisors, ACOAs can be tough bosses, difficult to work for and driving taskmasters. Because of their high need for control, they do not delegate easily. Sometimes, because of their need to be liked, they give mixed messages to employees. Said one employee of his manager in an aerospace company: "He gives me a job to do, but I know it is never mine. Even though he says it is 'my baby,' he is always looking over my shoulder."

ACOAs grew up in families in which they could not rely on their parents. They were always being let down. Perhaps this is the reason they are so untrusting of other employees and so controlling.

As we said, ACOAs tend to have high expectations of themselves; they are hard drivers. They bring the same energy into relationships with others. Because they are so out of touch with their feelings, and certainly not aware of others' feelings, they rarely realize the effects of their demands on those who work for them.

As supervisors, their problem is rarely with the job; their problems are almost always with the personnel. As managers they can evoke such hostility and create such friction that they make themselves and others miserable. Because of these feelings, and the experience of themselves as unsuccessful in their relationships with their employees, they can retreat into isolation and attempt to manage through impersonal rules and regulations.

As employees ACOAs have trouble with authority. Managers and supervisors are seen as surrogate parents, and ACOAs can unconsciously seek from them things they never received from a parent. The upheaval in their childhood home affects their reactions to supervisors in the present; ACOAs never knew how a parent was going to act, so when they hear that a boss wants to see them, they often panic.

Most of the things ACOAs want from their bosses they cannot expect to get in the corporate world. They want attention, encouragement, and approval for themselves as persons, not just their work, and they want to be able to see the boss as the perfect parent they never had. When the boss does not live up to these expectations, he or she is met with thinly disguised hostility and rejection. Unfortunately, as long as ACOAs do not go into their past to understand it and recover from it, bosses will frequently be objects of projection of much of the unresolved family material.

ACOAs tend to act dualistically toward bosses: either they adore them, giving over all their power, trying to meet their every wish, trying to be the favorite child, or they resist cooperating and become petulant children. ACOAs rarely act in a way that would be considered "normal" for the human organism—like asking questions when they do not understand something, speaking up if they think they see a better way of doing something, and setting reasonable limits on what they are willing to take on. Again, their problem is not in doing their job. They excel at tasks; it is the human relationships and the limits of their time and energy that are mysteries for the ACOA.

When we turn our attention to the means by which co-dependents replicate their dysfunctional systems in the organization, we see that they have many of the characteristics of the ACOA, as well as a constellation of behaviors that are unique to them.

CO-DEPENDENTS AT WORK

In organizations, the co-dependent relates to an addict in the same fashion that an enabler spouse relates to the addict in the family. Co-dependents tend to protect the addict and will cover for him or her when performance is questioned or appointments missed. Co-dependents, like ACOAs, are anxious around authority figures, but co-dependents tend to be compliant and to try to please, whereas ACOAs become resistant or defiant. Co-dependents avoid conflict at all costs. They avoid being a party to a conflict whenever possible. In fact, co-dependents are terrified of conflict; they are good peacemakers, as they are always attempting to bring others together.

Co-dependents have unusually high tolerance for confusion and crisis. Since confusion and crisis have been the norm of their daily lives, their meaning and identity come from being able to smooth things over and ease others' tension. They have come to see confusion as normal in their families and expect the same in the organization.

We saw one of the best examples of co-dependency when we were working as consultants for a division of a multinational corporation. In one of our first contacts with the divisional vice-president, we felt vaguely uncomfortable, because, as we conversed with him, it became apparent that he could not remember what he had said ten minutes earlier. This memory loss gave us little hope that he would be able to follow through on his commitments, or even remember that he had made them. What must it be like for his staff? Knowing that forgetfulness is one of the characteristics of an addict, we were alerted to this possibility and proceeded cautiously.

Our suspicions were confirmed when we spent time in

his office. Every time we visited his office we noticed that there were scores of liquor bottles on the desk and behind the desk. This was not a company given to much socializing at the office, so we realized we were indeed working with an active alcoholic. We raised our concerns with some of his co-workers. Immediately we could see their co-dependence activate. They told us that he was a good man and a fine person (we had no disagreement with this whatsoever). They told us that in the past, he had just been misunderstood, but now he just needed a chance to show what he could do. The behavior of his co-workers was another clue to us. Why were they so protective? Why did they need to be? We often find this kind of behavior in an alcoholic or addictive co-dependent setup, and the behavior of the co-dependents is as diagnostic as that of the addict. Subsequently, as a result of others' active denial, this man was promoted in his division.

The response of the co-workers was a good example of the disease of co-dependence and how it subtly supports the addictive system. When we raised the issue of the vice-president's alcoholism, the co-workers shifted the focus away from his disease to his being a good person. We had no quarrel with the fact that the vice-president was a good person: he was a good person with a disease that needed treatment. As they say in AA, "You are not a bad person getting good, you are a sick person getting well." By shifting the focus to his goodness, they did several things.

First, they became firmly entrenched in their denial system; they refused to let themselves see what was going on in front of them, thereby moving into the disease system themselves. Second, they enabled him to continue in his disease, a disease that is progressive and fatal; they covered for him and made excuses for him under the guise of caring.

Their final argument was that it would not be "Christian" to do an intervention with this man. They felt it would not be caring. Their caring was to take "care of." They did not realize that "caring for" would be to help him confront his disease, which was rendering him progressively ineffectual.

Co-dependents have quite a distorted view of caring. Co-dependents would rather care for someone in a way that leads to that person's death than to take the risk of seeing and speaking the truth and possibly offending him or her. Ultimately co-dependents are protecting themselves from the conflict that might ensue. Another issue for the co-dependent is that at some level of awareness, they know that when the addict begins recovery and no longer needs their "protection," they will have to find a new role and turn their gaze to themselves. They will have to deal with their disease and the loss of the rewards they get for being strong and indispensable.

Not all co-dependents are referenced solely to an addict. Co-dependents can replicate their dysfunctional family patterns and modes of response even when there is no addict available to be the recipient of their behaviors. This is because the co-dependent patterns are dysfunctionally functional for co-dependents. It is their way of being in the world, their identity.

We experienced the pervasiveness of co-dependence when we were conducting a workshop for a group of secretaries from a medical supply company; the women (there were no male secretaries in this company) were already self-identified co-dependents, so there was not the usual problem of denial in this group. However, some of the secretaries felt it was all right to be "nice" all the time. They often said, "No one likes a bitchy woman." At one point in the workshop, we broke into smaller groups of about twelve each, and various members of our team acted as facilitators in the smaller groups.

In one group, the facilitator noticed that the webbing in her chair was stretched and the chair cushion was slowly moving closer and closer to the floor. Jokingly, the facilitator mentioned this fact to the group. She said, "I seem to be sinking into the floor." Immediately, twelve women jumped out of their chairs and began scurrying around the room—some ran into the hallway in search of a replacement chair; others dashed to the facilitator to help her; and others offered their chairs. At that point, the facilitator asked everyone to stop and take a look at what she was doing. The defective chair had just provided a good lesson in co-dependent behavior.

Typical of co-dependents, these women had made several assumptions. They had not listened to the facilitator's actual words; they had decided what the facilitator really wanted: a chair. Even those who heard what she said jumped ahead and made an assumption about what was good for her. Being good co-dependents, they of course knew what the facilitator needed before she did. In the same fashion, these women leaped into action doing what they supposed would please the facilitator (co-dependents like to be liked; they search for ways to please). Throughout all of this activity, the needs of the facilitator became irrelevant; in fact, no one even thought to inquire whether she wanted a chair or was uncomfortable. Under the guise of being "nice," "unselfish," and "considerate of others" they had made the person they intended to serve invisible.

The facilitator explained she did not wish to have another chair; she was merely making an observation. She felt the chair would do just fine for the time being and if she needed another chair, she would get one herself or ask someone else for one.

The group was aghast that the facilitator was not asking for a chair and quite impressed that they had all had the same response. They also began to look at how often they "take over" other people by distorting what people say. They began to see how much interpretation they do of their bosses and how much they make assumptions about what managers want. They were getting a glimmer of the degree of self-centeredness that goes on under the guise of self-lessness. Some admitted they were more likely to want to help the facilitator than another group member because they saw the facilitator as an authority figure whom they wished to impress and please. This strongly suggests that co-dependents' "serving" of others often may be less altruistic than it appears. It is selectively focused on authority figures.

On page 49 we mentioned Robert Subby's nine "rules" of the dysfunctional addictive family system. We often find these rules operating in the organization as well: (1) it is not okay to talk about problems; (2) feelings should not be expressed openly; (3) communication is best if indirect, with one person acting as the messenger between two others; (4) be strong, good, right, and perfect; (5) make us proud; (6) don't be selfish; (7) do as I say and not as I do; (8) it is not okay to play or be playful; (9) don't rock the boat.

We saw some of these rules in operation in a mental health agency on the West Coast. A male unit director was sexually harassing several female staff members and clients, and propositioned them in one form or another. He promised the staff members raises and favorable evaluations if they would sleep with him. When women refused his favors, or when those who had become involved tried to break off their relationship, he threatened to fire them.

When several of them appealed to the executive director of the agency, he talked them out of bringing suit against the man, saying this was a critical time for the agency. He appeased the women with promises—he would "take care of this man," and if they could just wait, the man was "on his way out." Meanwhile, he extracted a promise from them not to talk about the "issue" at work.

Already several of Subby's rules are apparent. It was not all right to talk openly about the problem or express feelings. Furthermore, all communication between the women and the unit director became triangulated by going through the executive director. Thus, the unit director never got the full force of what the women were feeling about his behavior. Asking the women to refrain from bringing suit was a request to be strong, good, right, and perfect co-dependents, putting the reputation of the agency and the unit director above their needs as individuals and as women. By conforming to the rules, the women will not be seen as selfish; they did not rock the boat and the executive director could be proud of them for their restraint and cooperation.

You can see how seductive this is for a co-dependent or anyone else who grew up with these rules. What the executive director was asking felt "right" to some of these women—they had grown up with these rules and saw them as normal.

Unfortunately, the situation blew up in the face of the executive director when some incriminating letters from the unit director were made public. With the prospect of a suit looming against the agency, the director had to act fast and quickly fired the unit director (crisis orientation, perhaps).

Whenever co-dependents refuse to handle a situation as it comes along and deny what is really happening, they, by definition, push the matter to the point of crisis. In this case, the executive director responded to the situation in a mode characteristic of the co-dependent; that is, to control or to abandon. The director's attempts to control the situation failed miserably, so he literally abandoned responsibility and rode out the crisis as best he could. At the same time, he used the crisis as a convenient excuse for doing nothing more. He had already missed a chance to do an intervention with the unit director, an obvious sex addict, and had not made restitution to the affected staff and clients. Consequently, the unit director disappeared and may well be practicing his disease with other clients in some other part of the country. The women staff members have lost faith in the executive director, and the entire system has lost an opportunity to confront the issues, make an intervention, and learn about the organizational aspects of the disease of addiction and co-dependence.

The good co-dependent is adept at maintaining and perpetuating situations that should rightfully collapse. Remember that in the alcoholic family, the co-dependent enabler is the person who prevents the addict from feeling the full force of his or her behavior. The co-dependent keeps things tolerable—but at great cost to everyone.

For example, we once had the misfortune of using a retreat center in the Bahamas that was owned and operated by a full-blown co-dependent for our workshop. We arrived at the center, which had been described as "quaint," to find the place was literally falling down around us. The conditions were truly miserable, with rats running around the meeting room, doors falling off hinges, and dirt everywhere. Of course, the participants and staff at our workshop began requesting some rudimentary services and supplies, such as toilet paper. In true co-dependent fashion, the director agreed to every request and then filled none of them.

Co-dependents believe that if they just say yes, you will go away and they will not have to bother with what they have agreed to. They frequently say yes when they mean no because they want to be liked and avoid conflict. They have little awareness that in the normal system, people agree to things they are capable of doing and plan to do, and then they keep their word. In the co-dependent experience the addict makes hundreds of promises and breaks them daily, so this process of perpetual agreement to requests with no intention of following through is typical of their experience.

In fact, the retreat center director could not possibly meet most of the requests of our group. However, he could not risk experiencing the anger of the group, so he lied and then made himself scarce. He did not tell our group he could not meet their needs, thus giving them the opportunity to deal with reality and meet their own needs. That is co-dependence on the individual level; this story has another level, the organizational level.

As it happened, our retreat center director was a financial partner with seven people who had put up the money to purchase the land and buildings. Of course, with the place in such disrepair they could not hope to attract enough customers to meet expenses, much less generate money for capital improvements. The other partners were not willing to invest more money; thus, the director put himself in the position of lying to potential customers about the condition of the place in a desperate attempt to get business. Consequently, he almost killed himself (his health and financial status were both endangered) running around trying to keep the place from falling down and to respond to legitimate requests from his guests.

As long as he persisted in this behavior, he shielded the other partners from the reality of their investment. There are many ventures that should fold rather than limp along. This clearly was one of them. The payoff for the director was that all the partners recognized him as a virtual martyr, a nice guy and someone they could not get along without. He became indispensable. We have also noticed on subsequent trips to the area where this retreat center is located that he is haggard and appears to have aged dramatically in the last three years. Such is the life of the co-dependent.

Another example we encountered was a group of co-dependents who protected a key manager in a corporation, but the outcome was vastly different. This corporation was an international human services corporation. There was a department chief whose daily functioning was becoming progressively eccentric in a way that affected the entire department. According to people who knew him at home and at work, his behavior at home was similar to his behavior at work, and generally, his wife just put up with him. At work, however, things were not going so well. In the course of one year, four secretaries had come and gone, and the department was complaining about his behavior (never discussed directly with this man). In doing an organizational analysis of this situation, it became clear to us that the chief was thoroughly enmeshed in the addictive process. Most of the individuals in the organization had come together in such a way that they would not let him fall to the mercy of his own devices.

In looking at the situation more carefully, we realized that this man's position in the organization was so key and his power in outside networks so secure that he was not likely to lose his job as a consequence of his actions. It would not be organizationally feasible to move or terminate him. Furthermore, he was very insecure personally, and his denial system around his addiction was extremely solid. He was not open to any kind of personal change. It was at this point that the co-dependents had a key role.

Instead of working with the manager, we decided to focus attention on the rest of the department. The co-dependents were sufficiently miserable that they were open to looking at their part in the problem. They then began to understand their behavior and to name their characteristic functioning as co-dependence. They confronted their denial system in relation to their part in supporting his disease. As a last phase, they began to change their behavior in relation to the department chief. One example of this change occurred during tax time, which was usually a time of high stress for everyone. This was when the chief became most overbearing, tended to storm out of his office and made unreasonable demands on the secretaries. Before they became aware of their co-dependent behavior, the secretaries would scurry around, accede to his every request, and stay late to accomplish tax work that should have been done weeks earlier. They never voiced their resentment or their own needs. After the consultation they walked away when he started shouting, insisted upon advance notice when overtime was required, and generally refused to enter into the confusion. This chief gradually realized that he could not intimidate his immediate work group, and his behavior modified somewhat.

Although he still persists in his addictive and eccentric behavior, one part of the system has become healthier, and those around him are recovering from many of their symptoms of depression, migraine, insomnia, and stress related to work. It is likely that this man will not have a group willing to cover for him, if and when his behavior leads to serious trouble. Though the work group is not strong enough yet to do an intervention with this man, we now feel it is a possibility, and we will continue to explore that possibility with them.

A fine example of institutionalized co-dependence is drawn from our experience in consulting with a national service organization. We were hired to study decision making as it operated throughout the organization. Our task was to research and discover whether the process enhanced pluralism by including all people, especially women and minorities, or did it produce unnecessary conflict and exclusion of certain groups.

When we presented the results of our study, which showed that the decision-making process did indeed exclude significant portions of the membership of the organization and heighten conflict, it was initially well received, and then it was shelved. The committee that hired us admitted that our findings were not a shock to them and that our recommendations were sensible and to the point. They also felt the recommendations were in keeping with the mission and commitment of the organization. However, they felt the system could not tolerate the amount of change that would be necessary to follow all the recommendations and allow full participation by all people.

The co-dependent element here was that those in the decision-making position were not willing to risk the ire of powerful elements of the organization in order to make the organization congruent with its own mission and purpose. It was interesting to us that the committee would not act on our findings, because at the very time we were reporting our research, the entire organization was undergoing a massive change of its entire structure.

It is characteristic of co-dependents, especially those in decision-making positions, to back away from tough stands. Even though the entire philosophy of the organization is behind them, they abhor the disapproval of others and the conflict significant change requires. In organizations that are recovering from the addictive system and in healthy organizations, people in decision-making positions are willing to make effective, if unpopular, decisions. Their sense of self-worth comes not solely from being liked by others but also from doing what they know to be the right thing.

One of the easiest and clearest places where we can see the family rules operating in the workplace is in a family-run business. In this kind of business, the dynamics become even more intense.

We know a small family-owned and -operated chain of hardware stores in the Northeast whose board of directors is mostly family members. The family has been dysfunctional for years and has barely been able to negotiate their day-to-day living. Now we find them assigning and playing out in the corporation the same roles they have in the family system. They translate all the dysfunction to another level, the corporation and the board. Upon observing their board meetings, one of our consultants confessed he did not know whether he was at a board meeting or a brawl. The content was different; the context was different; and the process remained the same. Even the family roles remained the same.

The addictive system's process of the promise figured prominently in this family's decision to form a family corporation. They were aware that they were a troubled family, yet they believed a new project would give them a new chance to "make it" together. They resolved to do the business of the corporation differently. They wanted to make up for some of the mistakes of the past. Notice how familiar this sounds; this is the story of every addict, "Tomorrow things will be different."

At first, the excitement of starting up the business took

their attention away from their personal dynamics. It carried them on a wave of optimism. As the initial phase faded, it became a business, and the perennial dysfunctional patterns returned. Unfortunately, now the stakes were higher, because everyone had contributed significant amounts of money to the business. The business, per se, became a mirror of the family and was in grave trouble when we were called in.

We felt this was a good example of how wishing that patterns will change is not enough. Dysfunctional family patterns are part of the disease of the addictive system; they are not patterns that vanish because of wishes or goodwill.

In another family business, one that has been in operation for two generations, all the men are given significant roles and all the women are systematically ignored. Consequently, there is only one woman who still relates to the family business in any way. The one remaining woman is a major stockholder, but she is never notified about the shareholders' meeting. Whenever company business comes up, the brothers will speak to their sister's husband and refuse to deal with her. When she recently appeared at a shareholders' meeting (one she was not supposed to know about), her brothers and father were extremely uncomfortable and assigned her to a decorating job on a new project.

This is an example of a dysfunctional family that is also sexist. In this family the business practices, whose roots are in generations of family dysfunctioning, keep feeding back into the family dynamics, so that the family relations are fractured and unhappy most of the time.

From these two examples, it is easy to see why a new field of consulting to family business has arisen. In consulting to family businesses, it is absolutely essential to see that dysfunctional family patterns are repeatedly replicated in the business. Given the high percentage of dysfunctional families, one should always be alert to these patterns. In fact, family businesses are the best example of what we mean by the processes of addictive disease replicating itself in the workplace. When people do not actively recover from their addictive patterns, they are powerless to do anything but repeat the patterns wherever they go.

Sometimes the organization sets up addictive patterns and then the patterns go the other way, back to the family. We were reminded of this recently when we were reading about the divorce of a prominent industrialist and his wife of less than a year. Apparently, the new bride refused to be a quiet, traditional wife, content to be at her husband's side. The industrialist, who was accustomed to giving the orders and being the "man of the house," balked at his new wife's behavior. With almost no warning, he served her with divorce papers. Here is a man who believed he could run a marriage the way he ran his company. "When you have a liberated wife, you cannot simply give her orders like you can to a guy installing windshield wipers on the production line," said a friend of the family. "His problem is that he tries to treat her like an employee, not a partner."

Since the addictive system is all around us, we can become immersed in its behavior and its system in the workplace and in the family. These patterns are interactive. Some people are more affected by their life in organizations, others by their families. They feed into one another. This observation has been important in our work with organizations and individuals. Years ago, Schaef, who then had a large psychotherapy practice, noted that a major problem in relationships between men and women occurred when men tried to use in their marriages the same highly touted skills that were so successful in their corporations. These attempts were always disastrous for the relationship.

As we have seen women moving into corporations, we have seen them falling into the same patterns as the men Schaef observed earlier. We realized what we were seeing was not a gender-specific problem. As both men and women tried to use the skills they learned in addictive organizations, these same skills were found to be always counterproductive in their families and in their personal relationships.

For years, we thought we were seeing an issue peculiar to couples and couples therapy. Not until we understood the concept of the addictive organization did we see the whole scope of the problem and that these difficulties do indeed go both directions and feed into one another.

3. The Organization as the Addictive Substance

As we began recognizing the addictive process in organizations, we started to share our observations with those who attended our workshops and training groups. The sharing was always exciting. Frequently a discernible hush would fall over the group as we described the characteristics of addicts, ACOAs, and co-dependents in the workplace. Their eyes would light up, heads would nod, and a look of recognition would cross their faces. By the end of our discussion, people would be saying, "You've described where I work; I feel as if you've been in there with me." We learned much from these groups; they often volunteered examples and elaborated on our ideas based on their own experience in organizations.

For a while we continued describing addictive characteristics, believing the organization was just another context in which addictive behavior occurred. We had observed, studied, worked with, and experienced personally the effects of addiction on individuals and on families. It seemed logical to us that organizations provided just another context where people acted out their disease and were enmeshed by their own disease and that of others.

We recently began to realize we were seeing something more than the organization as a setting for addictive behavior: in many instances, the organization was itself the addictive substance. It was both setting *and* substance. This realization gave us an entirely new perspective on the addictive organization and moved us to another level of understanding of both addictions and organizations. In this chapter we describe how the organization functions as an addictive substance; we use workaholism as a key example.

Nothing in and of itself is addictive. *Anything* can be addictive when it becomes so central in one's life that one feels that life is not possible without the substance or the process. Organizations function as the addictive substance in the lives of many people. We recognized that for many people, the workplace, the job, and the organization were the central foci of their lives. Because the organization was so primary in their lives, because they were totally preoccupied with it, they began to lose touch with other aspects of their lives and gradually gave up what they knew, felt, and believed.

In the 1960s, the "company man" was the term for the man (mostly) who identified completely with the company. We have known of this phenomenon for years, but how was the organization itself functioning in such a way that it made itself an addictive substance in the lives of some employees? We were looking at a phenomenon at least one step beyond the company man.

One of the most important ways the organization functions as an addictive substance is through the promise it makes and holds out to every employee. Remember that the purpose of the promise in the addictive system is to take one out of the here and now. This process moves the person from what he or she knows, and fosters looking outside the self for answers, security, and a sense of worth.

The organization holds lots of promises. It promises that you will get ahead. It promises power, money, and influence. It promises that you will be a nice guy or gal if you perform

in certain ways. If you live up to what the company promotes, you may even be liked and "belong."

Almost all the promises of the organization are linked to
the promises of the society. They are the same: power, influence, and money. They are the good life as defined by the
popular culture and by advertising. This is seductive.

The promise of the good life keeps us actively focused
on the future in the belief that even if things are not so good
now, they will get better. The future orientation of the
promise in the organization is one of the processes that
prevent us from looking at the present functioning in the
system and seeing it for exactly what it is, addictive. People
often feel stuck in organizations. Rather than acknowledging their feelings, they find it easier to look forward to the
weekend, a vacation, or retirement. By continuing to present
us with the promise, the organization remains central in our
lives, in control of our present, and "hooks" us into an
addictive relationship with the organization, the giver of the
promise.

Some organizations promise things people longed for in
their families and never did get, like recognition, approval,
the development of social skills, and caring. "We are one big,
happy family here," a software executive said of his company. "We socialize on Friday nights. We play ball together.
We know each other's spouses. We help each other out."
"Oh," we said, "and what do you do when someone doesn't
want to socialize or gets out of line?" "They don't stay
around long," said the executive.

This was an organization in which the best-adjusted employees were the ones who had come from dysfunctional
homes and were willing to let the company become their
family. Those who had no family came to believe that family consisted of the types of activities promoted in the or-

ganizational family. They let this model feed back into their primary families. Those who did not feel so comfortable being included in the wide arm of the corporation, whose spouses and children resisted company picnics and wearing company T-shirts, always felt uneasy, usually did not readily "move up" in the company, or left.

Those who looked to the company and believed it was a family were hooked by a very seductive promise indeed. For what kind of a family can the organization possibly be?

It is a family in which membership is dependent on playing by rather rigid rules and behaving according to established norms. This kind of corporation is a "family" whose main mode of operating is control. Thus, acceptance in the family is won by learning the right thing to do and doing it (just as in the addictive family). The main thing learned about family from the promise of the organization is that membership is conditional upon not being oneself and following one's own path. The other lesson learned is to keep attuned outside oneself and to be constantly vigilant about those things one needs to do to stay in the company's good graces and win approval. So the promise of the organization to provide family feeling is a promise based on control and dependent on one's staying out of touch with one's own needs. In this, the corporation is just like an addictive, dysfunctional family.

Another area where we see the organization's promise operating is in its mission and goals. All organizations have a mission; it is their public statement for why they exist. Presumably all employees are oriented toward the accomplishment of the mission and the purpose. Companies with unclear missions often flounder helplessly, because they have no sense of why they exist or the meaning of their work.

Although we have worked with myriad types of organizations, we find those in the "helping" professions—hospitals, schools, agencies, churches, and community organizations—have the most difficulty with the promise of the mission. The reason many people are attracted to the helping professions is that they identify with, and sincerely believe in, the stated goals of the organizations they join, as well as with the professions with which they are identified. However, often what they are committed to and what they experience are quite different.

We'll use as an example a group of nurses with whom we once worked in a large metropolitan hospital. At one point in our work with them, it became clear they were confused and angry about their work. Since this confusion and anger seemed to relate to what they seemed to think they should be doing and what they actually were doing, as an experiment we asked them to list the stated goals of the hospital. The goals they listed were concerned with promoting health and wellness, being responsive to the needs of the people, providing high-quality health care, and developing new forms of healing. They all felt comfortable with these goals. We then asked them to list the unstated goals of the hospital. The unstated goals turned out to be saving the city money, being a vehicle for the political advancement of hospital administrators, upholding the reputation of the hospital, and increasing federal funding. Inevitably, the accomplishment of the unstated goals was where they spent most of their time. They had joined the hospital to work toward the stated goals, yet in reality, most of their time was spent working toward the unstated goals. No wonder they were confused, frustrated, and angry. They felt misled and used. They had been promised something that was a "con."

The power of the promise is that it seems possible, just possible enough to keep people hooked in.

This "con" was also true in the national service organization referred to earlier, whose stated goal was to include all people in decision making. But, in fact, the unstated goals were, Don't rock the boat, Don't introduce wide change in the system, and Don't ask us to operate congruent with our stated principles of pluralism.

Is it any wonder people in the helping professions are often exhausted and depressed? They join an organization to do one thing and spend most of their time doing another. As we see, frequently the thing they end up doing is totally incongruent with the reasons they became helpers in the first place.

The organization becomes the addictive substance for its employees when the employees become hooked on the promise of the mission and choose not to look at how the system is really operating. The organization becomes an addictive substance when its actions are excused because it has a lofty mission. We have found an inverse correlation between the loftiness of the mission and the congruence between stated and unstated goals. When this lack of congruence exists, it is more probable that the organization will enter into a rigid denial system with concomitant grandiosity.

Schaef states that grandiosity is one of the characteristics of the addictive system. In this case, grandiosity refers to pretending to be more or something other than what one is. It is gross self-importance. Grandiosity keeps the mission lofty and frequently unattainable. We have found that the helping professions often refuse to make their statement of purpose realistic. This we believe is partially because of their inability to deal with the feelings of pain and frustration they experience when they see so few real changes. It is also probably because improvement of the kind they seek by its very nature proceeds in small increments: they, after all, work with human beings.

The grandiosity of the mission is a fix. It can reassure us that we are important and do important work. This is its purpose.

We know of another health corporation that has a stated mission to minister to the health care needs of the poor. When they were pressed on their unimpressive record, they rationalized that their mission was actually to the spiritually poor, not to the materially poor. This is quick thinking, a self-deluded statement, a "con."

Addicts are consummate cons. Initially their con looks good to others; unfortunately, they usually end up conning themselves as well. They come to believe their own lie. The promise of the mission is the same process. The very fact of *having* goals frequently can be enough to con employees into believing that everything is all right in the organization. The mission is like a household god. As long as it is in its shrine, the organization is protected, even if what it is doing has little to do with the stated mission.

Whenever the promise of the mission puts a buffer between the people in the organization and what is really happening in the organization, the addictive process is flourishing. Then a useful vehicle, which potentially has great integrity for the employees, has been turned into an addictive substance. One of the ways employees react to this addictive process is by changing their perceptions and thinking, therefore deluding themselves. They try to make themselves believe that the stated mission of the organization is really what is happening, even if what they are seeing and feeling as they work is quite different. When organizations function as the addictive substance, it is in their interest to keep promoting the vision of the mission, because as long as the employees are hooked by it, they are unlikely to turn their awareness to the present discrepancies. They choose to stay numb in order to stay in the organization. The mission is a powerful source of identification for workers. It is a type of philosophical orientation that appeals to their values. Through the mission they find a link between themselves and the organization.

In addition to the mission, there are other more concrete processes by which employees stay hooked into the company. These are the processes by which the organization keeps itself central in the lives of its employees. Loyalty and the benefits of loyalty are other paths to the organization becoming an addictive agent or "fix."

There is nothing inherently wrong with being loyal to an organization or being a dedicated employee. In fact, this is essential for a good working relationship. However, loyalty to the organization becomes a fix when individuals become preoccupied with maintaining the organization. When loyalty to the organization becomes a substitute for living one's own life, then the company has become the addictive substance of choice. The organization itself has ways of enhancing its centrality in workers' lives, primarily through processes like benefits, bonuses, tenure, and rewards.

We want to say here that we are not opposed to benefits and retirement packages for workers. We believe benefits are important and necessary for workers and that too few workers have adequate benefits. The issue is not benefits per se, but the way the organization and individuals use them to stay central in the lives of workers and consequently to prevent people from moving on and doing what they need to do. When the benefits become a controlling factor in one's life the organization becomes the addictive agent. It is when the organization is willing to take advantage of the worker's dependence and not be competitive with other workplaces for the worker's loyalty and creativity that the organization functions as the addictive agent.

A good example of the addictiveness of benefits was provided by a man who came to one of our men's workshops. This man, who has lived most of his life in a major industrial city, was aghast to hear other men in the group say such things as "I've been at my present job long enough, I need to move on to something else" or "I feel unchallenged and bored at work, I'm looking to begin another career" or "I think it is time my family and I moved on and experienced a new part of the country." Our participant was shocked. In fact, he said in his social circle in the city where he lived, no one ever expected to change jobs. They worked in the same company until retirement. The reason was that they did not want to lose their benefits. Happiness at the job or feeling good about their work did not figure into their decision to stay on. They needed the benefits; they lived for them; and they could not afford to leave the organization if it meant losing them. It was inconceivable that they would make mid-life career changes or consider what they really wanted to do.

Many people whom we have interviewed are completely burned out at their work. They may be sick or aging or simply unable to be creative in their field any longer. Most of these people want to be doing something else. When we challenge them to explore other opportunities, they respond that they cannot afford it. We should not miss the real message here: it is partially that they cannot afford to take the risk of being fully alive.

Benefits encourage dependency, and if workers lose all benefits when they leave a company, the company itself is then burdened with people who may be counterproductive because they do not want to be in the organization but are afraid to leave. In order to stay, they have to become not dead and not alive—zombies. The organization has become the addictive agent.

Like any addiction, the organization's benefits and bonuses become the controlling factor in the lives of employees. "Getting one's fix" becomes primary. We have an acquaintance who works as a sales rep in the highly competitive photocopier field. Every month he sets his own sales goals, and his team sets an overall goal. The purpose is to achieve ever-higher sales as individuals and as a group. There are substantial rewards in the form of bonuses, parties, and eventually vacations. The purpose of the rewards is to motivate these sales reps to sell more and more products. Our friend laughingly says that he sometimes finds himself selling customers products he knows they do not need in order to meet personal and team quotas. We know that addicts will stop at nothing to get a fix. Their behavior becomes increasingly more self-centered and personally immoral. These kinds of benefits function in the same way. The "fix" or rewards become primary, and the individual's ethics begin to recede into the background. This is what it means to be out of touch with one's personal morality and one's spirituality. It is what AA means by moral deterioration. The organization has become the source of moral deterioration as it makes itself indispensable in the lives of its employees through its structure of benefits, bonuses, and tenure. In this way it has become the addictive substance.

As we were pondering the implications of the organization as the addictive substance, we were contacted by a woman who had worked as an employee assistance program (EAP) counselor in a large utility company. We shared with her our realization that the organization could function as the addictive substance. Since she worked with many active addicts in their recovery within the company, we wondered how she would react to the implications of this idea in her company.

"Oh, yes," she responded. "The place I work does all the things you are describing, and it does even more." We asked her to elaborate. She described to us what happened one day when she went to work with a headache and was feeling slightly "down." She asked her supervisor for a few aspirin. The supervisor had no aspirin; instead, she offered the woman something called "greenies." Our friend took the pills and immediately felt better; in fact, she felt high. Upon investigation, she discovered that all the supervisors had "greenies" and they were instructed to hand them out to any employee who had any of a wide variety of complaints. "Greenies" were amphetamines—"speed." Coincidentally, our friend was a recovering alcoholic and overeater. If she had been a recovering drug addict, being offered "greenies" would have threatened her sobriety. As it was, she was only being invited to get hooked on drugs at work as part of company policy.

Here, the organization is both itself the addictive substance and is offering an addictive substance to employees to make them feel good. Numb people are less critical and less aware. They are also less alert. If you no longer feel blue or have a headache, then you can avoid having to ask yourself why the feelings were there in the first place. We can see the horrendous proportions of this disease when we see an organization distributing a habit-forming drug to employees, some of whom may already be substance abusers.

Sometimes the organization itself may use fixes to remain the primary fix in your life. This is the lesson from our friend's experience, and it gave us a new respect for the presence of and the acceptance of the addictive system in organizations.

We now move on to consider the prime mechanism for how the organization becomes the addictive substance in one's life. Of course work is the primary link one has with the organization. A fatal form of work in addictive organizations is what is called workaholism.

Our investigation of workaholism has been very instructive. It has shown us the extent of the denial operating around a particularly insidious form of the addictive disease.

The deliberate innocence about workaholism was evidenced by a statement a woman made to us at a training seminar. She is a recovering alcoholic, and she is quite open about her recovery with her family. She had been attempting to learn more about her family of origin so as to determine the roots of her alcoholism. In a conversation with her mother, she said, "Mom, am I the only alcoholic in the family?" Her mother responded immediately, "Of course you are, all the rest work hard." She *was* the only alcoholic; she was *not* the only addict.

To understand workaholism, one must penetrate an almost impenetrable wall of denial. When we went in search of information on workaholism, we discovered there were thousands of articles that had been written on stress and burnout. The focus of these articles was primarily stress reduction through exercise, diet, and changes in life-style. In a computerized search through several university libraries, we could find only ten books on workaholism, and only two of these were a serious treatment of the issue. We were incredulous. How could a topic that is clearly part of the popular culture, and a word everyone recognizes, be the subject of so little inquiry? And why were the inquiries that were made so frequently directed to treating the symptoms and not addressing the underlying disease process itself?

We began to see more and more evidence that the culture supports and promotes workaholism. We felt, for example, that many of the magazines for career women, like *Working Woman* and *Savvy*, touted the example of the workaholic woman. Articles on women who made their first million before the age of 30 are descriptions of superbeings who founded companies, jog and swim daily, put in sixty hours at the office, have a family and children, bring work home in the evenings, and work weekends. There is always some variation on the basic theme for the reader. The message is, "Work like this and you will get ahead."

Interviews in such magazines have women saying of themselves, "I am a workaholic, and I love it." With what other addictions can you say such a thing? Imagine a well-dressed executive saying in an interview, "I am an active alcoholic, and I love it." Imagine a bulimic or anorexic saying, "Vomiting ten times a day feels great—I recommend it."

Only a system that chooses to be deliberately blind to the effects of this disease and that is thoroughly into its denial in relation to it can tout workaholism as a condition to be emulated.

We see workaholism as an addictive process in which the addictive agent is work. The workaholic becomes addicted to the process of work, using it as a fix in order to get ahead, be successful, avoid feeling, and ultimately avoid living. Like all addictions, workaholism adversely affects families and personal relationships at home and on the job. It is a progressive disease that leads to death if not treated. The side effects of the stress of workaholism may be even more severe than the physical effects of alcoholism, for example, bringing about an even earlier death for some workaholics.

Work is a very tricky addiction, however, because when workaholics are most "into" their disease, they feel most alive, even though it may be killing them. In our interviews with workaholics, we have found that the fix may not be the work itself, but an adrenaline high that accompanies the work. Many workaholics describe the surge of energy they get from their work. They identify this surge with "feeling alive and energetic." They do not get the same surge on a family vacation or a night out with friends. In fact, they experience a total letdown and depression when they are not at work or thinking about work.

For people who are not work-addicted, there are pauses between projects, times when one savors success and rests and spends time with loved ones. For the workaholic, the prospect of these pauses is terrifying, for they are not experienced as times of release and quiet. They are times of being out of touch with the "fix" of the addictive substance and functioning in an arena that cannot be controlled by the work process.

Researchers working on stress have said that stress is life-threatening because the body was not built to withstand a constant rush of adrenaline. Adrenaline is the substance that allows us to do impossible physical feats in times of severe crisis. Stress researchers claim that modern life "tricks" the body into believing there is a constant crisis, with the result that we produce amazing amounts of adrenaline on a daily basis.

Stress research provides us with an interesting perception about workaholism. Many workaholics have taken the recommendations of stress researchers and exercise daily and eat right. This "healthiness" results in their being able to work even harder and thus maintain their addiction. Is it not interesting to see how this may be similar to the behavior of an alcoholic, who will do anything to protect his or her supply? The insidious thing is that their stress reduction activities appear to be promoting health when, in actuality, these activities only allow workaholics to prolong their addiction—taking the focus off their addiction, actually supporting their addiction, and serving as a con for themselves and others. It appears that stress research and stress reduction workshops may indeed actually be supporting the perpetuation of the addictive system.

Work addiction is also extremely destructive to families and personal relationships. When we listen to stories adult children tell of growing up in families with a workaholic parent, they sound identical to those of ACOAs. Said one woman of her experience:

> Everything revolved around my father's work. If we got too playful and made noise we would be quieted because Daddy was either working or sleeping. When work went poorly, he was moody, angry, and destructive. When it went well, he was jolly. We were constantly watching him to see what kind of day he had had so that we could act accordingly. We rarely saw him. Sometimes he stayed in the city overnight or on big projects, he would be gone for weeks at a time. Work was the overriding excuse for everything, family celebrations, plans and vacations all bowed to the demands of work. We could never count on anything. My father married his work and it had the excitement of a mistress. I don't think my mother or our family were ever second place in my father's life, I believe for him we didn't exist at all. I grew up spending inordinate amounts of time thinking about my father, yet never really knowing him. I hate him for this and I miss him deeply.

It should be noted that making a lot of money is not the purpose of workaholism. It is the actual *process of working* that is the fix, not the outcome. Like any addiction, work takes over one's life, it becomes primary, resulting in a loss of perspective on other realities. This is because the addictive process becomes its own reality. It is a closed system. There are many payoffs when the organization promotes workaholism. Certainly the most obvious is a core group of workers who are totally dedicated to the company.

We recently had lunch with a young man who is beginning a career with a major fashion designer. He seemed relieved to be spending time with us. When we asked him about his job, he said that he could only describe it as grueling. He said the hours were long and there was a lot of pressure. No one in this firm ever took a lunch break. Though time off for lunch was written into the personnel policies, he said he would be seen as lazy and not interested in furthering his career if he took even a half hour for lunch. In this company, the only way for a young designer to gain acceptance was to not go to lunch or take any breaks whatsoever during the day. Workaholism is the ticket into the group.

We find that workaholics frequently have a constellation of addictions. Their primary addiction is to work, and they also have secondary addictions to alcohol, food, drugs, or any of the other process or substance addictions described earlier.

The way the workaholic protects his or her supply is to take attention away from the primary disease of work. The secondary addictions act as crutches and smoke screens, allowing the denial system to remain intact. This keeps one from focusing on the main problem. Also, work addictions require a certain amount of conscious awareness to do the job and be successful at it. The role of the secondary addictions is to permit this focus, yet keep one's awareness just dull enough so that it is not attuned to the physiological and psychological pain of work.

We are reminded of this phenomenon by a man who was

a workaholic and a teacher. At the end of the week he would find himself completely worn out by his dedication to work and his overinvolvement in school activities. Also, by the end of the week he would be filled with questions about why he was continuing to work for the school system, why his philosophy of education conflicted with the administrator's, what education should be about anyway, and so on. Notice that these are important questions, not only for this teacher, but also for the school system itself.

At the end of the week, this teacher did not sit down and face his inner turmoil, nor did he share it with his colleagues. He went drinking. He spent Friday night and much of his weekend in a mild stupor. By Monday he was back at school, his inner questions quelled, and the pattern repeated itself week after week.

In some way, this pattern is ideal for an organization that wants cogs as workers. This man put superhuman effort into the system and never raised issues that were uncomfortable or challenging for the organization. A healthy organization relies on employees' ideas, and on conflicts and reactions as a rich source of continual change. In these areas, this man is a noncontributor at best, yet his single-minded dedication keeps him from being identified as a problem to himself or the system. His secondary addiction of drinking keeps him from noticing his work addiction. Also, his primary addiction is so socially acceptable that it keeps others in the system from seeing him for what he really is—an active addict, a man in distress, and a man who has a progressive, fatal disease.

Our interviews with workaholics and our experience with them in organizations have led us to the conclusion that the addictive organization needs workaholism and consequently rewards workaholic behavior. We have also concluded that workaholism is the most socially acceptable of the addictions because it is so socially productive. It has socially productive results. Many people have responded to our description of workaholism with statements like, "It is not the same as alcoholics, who destroy themselves and their loved ones; workaholics are productive members of the society."

We have to recognize that for some organizations and for some people, destroying one's life and loved ones is acceptable if one produces something useful in the society. And that, of course, is what a workaholic does. It is also interesting to see another process of the addictive system at work. In the addictive system, if one can find anything at all wrong with a person or an idea, that person or idea can be completely dismissed. The inverse is also true. Hence, if one good thing can be found about workaholism, then the whole process is "good."

Since we have worked with many church organizations, it is difficult for us to miss the role of the church in actually promoting workaholism. Theologically and in practice, the church puts before us the picture of the good Christian as one who works hard. The good martyr is the typical co-dependent who works selflessly for others and never attends to his or her own needs. We have heard of "designer drugs"; workaholism may be the designer drug for the church as well as for the corporation.

We believe that denial about workaholism is so pervasive because underneath this addiction is an attachment no one is willing to face; it is the attachment to an economically based system, capitalism, and a social structure that undergirds this system. We believe that the Protestant work ethic and Christian religions support both.

We have been impressed with the role of workaholism in the loss of spiritual values in the society and in the organization. Addictions lead to the loss of spirituality and to loss of touch with one's own morality. We were interested that many workaholics described their immersion in their work as a kind of altered state, much like one experiences with drugs. We soon saw that this altered state experienced in work was the adrenaline high. As we probed further, we realized that the altered state one experiences at work really acts as a mood-altering drug and removes one from the reality of the present, thus creating a feeling of transcendence. It is a delusion that keeps the person in the addictive process and longing for more. Sadly, the feeling of transcendence actually causes the loss of spirituality—while feeding the illusion that it is itself something akin to spirituality.

The addictive organization promotes workaholism. It loves it as the "cleanest" of addictions. Unlike drug- or alcohol-addicted people, workaholics rarely miss a day (they just drop dead). Like good ACOAs and co-dependents, workaholics can be counted on to go the extra mile; they rarely let you down.

All the experiences we have charted here—the promise of the organization, the mission, the benefits, the distributing of addictive drugs to employees, and the support for workaholism—are all ways the organization positions itself as central in the lives of employees and becomes the addictive agent. In each we saw people who became progressively dependent on the organization and could not function without the organization. It was in seeing this that we had to admit that the organization itself had indeed become an addictive substance.

4. The Organization as Addict

The fourth way addictions operate in the organizational set-ting is a way that is pervasive and has many far-reaching implications. It is absolutely essential that we recognize that *organizations themselves are addicts,* and they function corporately the same way any individual addict functions. We came to this understanding by asking ourselves what we know about addicts.

In addition to the characteristics and processes we have described earlier, we know that addicts are people

whose lives have become unmanageable and who are pow-erless over their addictive behavior

who have become increasingly involved in the addictive process

whose lives have become dominated by their addictions and who have lost a sense of their values and personal morality

who function primarily out of characteristics such as self-centeredness, the illusion of control, dishonesty, and dualism

who become progressively isolated from input from society, family, and friends

who, as they become internally more chaotic, exert progres-sively more control over those on whom they depend and on their immediate surroundings whose thinking process is confused, obsessive, and paranoid-like and different from normal thinking processes

The more time we spent with organizations that initially were thought to be "troubled or dysfunctional," the more we realized that these organizations were functioning in much the same manner as the addict we have just described. We feel that there is no real possibility for change and transformation in the organization unless those involved recognize that they are addictive and function the same as an active addict. In fact, we believe that the key to organizational transformation lies in this truth. Understanding the intricacies of the organization as addict is a good example of the hologram at work. It is easy to see at the organizational level what we have seen at the individual level. The addictive organization is a natural outgrowth of the people who are in it and the society in which it is embedded.

We know, because of our work with addicts, that they may get temporary relief from psychological intervention, but their disease is progressive, and they eventually have to face the addictive disease in order to recover. Psychological techniques and solutions can go only so far and are only superficially helpful. When an organization is an addict, it is necessary to acknowledge and work with this first before engaging in any other form of organizational development.

This chapter explores the concept that the organization is an addict. It delves into such organizational variables as communications, thinking, management and personnel processes, as well as structural components. Through this model we find that though the form of addictiveness may be different in organizations, the basic disease remains the same as we see in the individual and must be addressed for recovery to take place.

COMMUNICATIONS PROCESSES

Because communication is so basic and so central to organizational functioning, it is very sensitive to any type of dysfunction. In many organizations, people admit they have communication problems. We would not dispute that. Communications are usually terrible in a dysfunctional organization, but they are also more likely the symptom of a larger, more pervasive problem. Let us look at some of the typical ways communication functions in the addictive organization.

Communication in the addictive organization is frequently *indirect.* This indirectness takes many forms. People who feel they have conflicts with one another refuse to state their conflicts openly to the person concerned. They are also unwilling to discuss these conflicts in a group setting. Instead, they avoid the significant parties, carry tales to others, and spend inordinate amounts of time justifying their position. They discuss the conflict with persons who can lend a sympathetic ear and who are often powerless to do anything other than listen. (We realize here that it is tempting to say that this is just how people function. It is not how people function; it is the way people have learned to function in an addictive system.)

Indirectness does not exist only in relation to conflict. Communication in these settings is usually *vague, confused, and ineffective.* Communication in an addictive organization is often characterized by abundant production of paper memos. We once watched a maintenance man who needed to be reimbursed seven dollars for delivering some materials spend one hour going to eight different persons to sign the voucher so he could get his money. Complex procedures often mask an inability to communicate.

Written memos are frequently used in addictive organizations to avoid face-to-face confrontation on touchy issues. Sometimes memos are the main mode of communication in larger companies, leading to feelings of isolation. Since addicts cannot be trusted to communicate clearly or remember what is communicated, memos have become a necessity and functional.

Triangulation is a characteristic process of addictive communication. If Joe wants to get a message to Sue, he does not speak to Sue, call Sue, or send her a direct memo. He asks Mary to tell her. Except for routine messages, Joe uses triangulation because he does not want to come into direct contact with Sue. He does not want to face her disappointment, refusal, or questions. Joe is aware that he has feelings when he faces Sue directly. Rather than deal with those feelings, he avoids them and gets someone else to do his work. The "someone else" becomes a good co-dependent the minute he or she agrees to relieve Joe of the task he needs to do himself, and Joe becomes dependent on cooperation, translation, and so on. We realize that in large corporations, communication cannot always be direct. This is not what we are discussing here. We are talking about those instances in which direct communication is indicated and would be more efficient and helpful.

There is a lot of *gossip* in addictive organizations. Sometimes there is gossip because there is very little communication in any direction. When there is no functional direct communication, one hears about change from those who know the gossip. The purpose of gossip is to excite and titillate, as well as to establish a seat of power. It usually produces paralysis, because sources cannot be revealed, and real information is always obfuscated. Gossip helps to avoid real, direct, and effective communication. It relieves tension while providing a feeling of intimacy. In the end it is ephemeral.

Secrets operate in much the same way as gossip, except that secrets usually come from reliable sources. There are many secrets in addictive organizations. Secrets are usually "for their own good." Decisions about money, salary, and personnel are often secret. Secrets are information being managed that is not open to all. Our friend from the utility company was frequently let in on company secrets. She always felt privileged to receive the secrets; it engendered a sense of power in her. She believed that "knowledge was power," even though she could do nothing with or about the information she received. There is a saying in Al-Anon that families are only as sick as the secrets they keep—so too in organizations. Secrets are divisive and powerful. Keeping them is difficult, fosters dishonesty, endangers trust, and creates "in" groups and tension. Organizations moving toward health try to keep fewer secrets and ideally work toward none at all.

Another form of communication in addictive organizations is what Chris Argyris calls *"skilled incompetence."*[1] This refers to the phenomenon of executives who are skilled communicators, highly committed and respected by each other, using communication skills (much like disinformation?) to cover up real problems.

These executives meet repeatedly to brainstorm and develop strategy. Yet when they meet, they always seem to go in circles. They make endless lists of agenda items on the flip charts and put check marks next to the important items, and in the end, everyone leaves feeling exhausted having accomplished little. Argyris says that these executives were skilled, but their skills were being used to avoid upset and conflict at meetings; consequently, they did not say what they mean, nor were they open to test the assumptions about the group's ability to deal with or utilize conflict. Their very communication skills inhibited a resolution of the important issues in the meeting.

The avoidance of conflict and of difficult issues can be institutionalized and lead to a corporate environment that cannot tolerate "straight talk," honesty, or directness. In the addictive organization, there is little or no straight talk. The culture of the addictive organization is one of confusion and chaos. According to Argyris, there are four easy steps to chaos.[2] The first step is to design an obviously ambiguous statement that the receiver recognizes as ambiguous but does not question. The second step is to ignore any inconsistencies in the message. Next is to make the ambiguity and inconsistencies undiscussable and, finally, to make the undiscussability, undiscussable.

Argyris believes that such chaos is part of a defensive routine that has become systemic. As routines becomes norms, more and more people in the organization begin operating out of them. In this kind of setup, people can leave the organization and new ones arrive, but the routines remain intact.

We agree with Argyris that the culture of chaos remains intact in organizations and becomes systemic. We think, however, that he misses the root cause of its stability. We believe it is because the organization has become an addictive system and has that disease process underlying *the defensive routine.* When one works with addicts, it is easy to see that this behavior is clearly characteristic of addiction.

Thus far we have been discussing the process of communication in addictive organizations. We now want to say something about the *content* of communication. Addictive organizations are skilled at eliminating significant communication. Significant communication is any information that could make employees more effective, decisions more strategic, and change more likely in the organization. The processes we have been describing serve to cloud significant information and make it more difficult to get access to what is really going on. Consequently, mundane announcements may be given more time at meetings than important decision making. Significant content simply does not get through in an addictive organization. We are not saying that this is malicious or deliberate. What we are saying is that this blocking of significant information is observably present in addictive organizations.

The expression of feelings is also noticeably absent in addictive organizations. Frozen feelings are institutionalized. First of all, feelings are just not discussed in these companies. If there is a display of feelings, it is seen as inappropriate. A common statement is, "Get control of yourself." There is a general belief that if feelings are expressed, one will be seen as unstable, and this could jeopardize one's security on the job.

In the addictive organization, people are either *out of touch* with what they feel, or they *put down* any feelings or awareness of what they need, because to have feelings or to need something would be seen as being out of control. We often encounter executives who are not aware when they need to take time off. In these organizations it is seen as inappropriate for other executives to observe that a co-worker seems to need a vacation. This is a good example of the lack of intimacy in the addictive organization and the unwillingness to honor feelings.

By intimacy we are not referring to sexual intimacy or even what might be seen as emotional intimacy. What we mean by intimacy is the willingness to know oneself and to let oneself be known by others. William Ouchi describes intimacy as a common thread binding people together in caring closeness and support in social relations. He observes that intimacy is very rare in American life and that we resist the notion that closeness can be achieved in a workplace. We have segmented our lives in such a way that personal feelings have no place at work. Interestingly, the inability to form and maintain intimacy is a prime characteristic of an addict. We do not feel that it is by accident that our corporations have been structured to reflect this lack of intimacy.

In the addictive organization, the prohibition against being who you are makes intimacy almost impossible. The addictive organization then tries to counteract this reality by setting up planned encounters and workshops in which individuals tell one another what they like and dislike about the other and practice "communication skills." Regardless of how many communication workshops the organization sponsors, intimacy is not possible, because the person and the system are part of the same disease. We know that maintaining this disease is dependent upon keeping out of touch personally and institutionally, and a quick "communications fix" may bring temporary relief, but it does not address the problem.

The addictive organization has a narrow view of the type of content that is acceptable inside the organization. Most of the content communicated must be *logical and rational.*

We were reminded of this problem when hearing the testimony of the scientists and engineers who worked with the ill-fated spaceship *Challenger.* Apparently, some of those closest to the project had enough information to be sincerely worried about the worthiness of the spacecraft. Others just "felt" it shouldn't be sent up. However, in the NASA community hunches and intuitions were not considered reliable content for a decision to curtail the flight. Feelings, intuitions, and imagination are considered illegitimate and not controllable. Consequently, feelings and intimacy are just not acceptable. The information that gets through has to come through the indirect, triangulated, and defensive communication forms. Ironically, there is a belief that feelings and intimacy are counterproductive to the accomplishment of the task. We have known for some time in organizational circles that attending to the process usually facilitates production. We have seen that the really addictive organizations are noticeably depressed and entropic and have difficulty in attending to tasks except at crisis times.

Since the acceptable kinds of content for communication in the addictive organization are logical and rational statements, let us look at the thinking processes in the addictive organizations to understand better how they operate.

THINKING PROCESSES

Loss of corporate memory, or forgetfulness, is an outstanding characteristic of the addictive organization. People have said of addicts that they cannot learn from their past behavior, because they have no memory. This is one of the aspects of the disease. Addictive organizations have the same problem.

Forgetfulness among employees is certainly related to the sheer amount of work and the confusing way communication occurs. Sometimes memory is very selective. A man who worked for a heavy equipment manufacturer told us he was part of an executive team that had responsibility for marketing strategies. They met routinely in a team of seven. Over time they discovered they did well acknowledging small tasks and completely forgot large, important projects. This even happened when tasks had definite deadlines. "I know it is hard to believe," he said. "But we just spaced it."

This is not unusual in the addictive organization. Small tasks suddenly become more attractive. They appear manageable with the depleted human and organizational resources available, whereas big tasks are overwhelming and are just ignored or forgotten.

This type of forgetfulness may be related to the penchant of addicts, co-dependents, and the addictive institutions to take on what they cannot do but believe they should accept. In the case of the executive just mentioned, his team was overloaded with work because a co-dependent team leader took on more work than he could possibly do. Instead of dealing with the conflict among themselves about work loads, they conveniently avoided the task by forgetting it.

Another aspect of forgetfulness we see related to organizations is not learning from past mistakes and past experience. Occasionally, in our role as consultants we will remind people that they are proposing an organizational design or project they used in the past with dubious results. No one remembers. Sometimes groups get into the middle of a project, and someone has a feeling that "we have been through this before." Not until they are too deeply committed to back out do they see that they are replicating old patterns and old solutions.

Addictive organizations get into their most serious trouble when they forget to keep the primacy of their mission before them. They then lose contact with the reason for their existence, the contribution they expect to make to the society or what they want to do. Although it seems incomprehensible that organizations could be so out of touch, the confusion in the addictive organization often results in the company's pursuing a product line or strategy that looks good in the abstract at the moment without asking how it relates to mission, consumer needs, or readiness. They then end up having to develop a market. Addictive organizations are always on the lookout for the "quick fix," and anything that may provide temporary relief or solutions is leaped upon gladly, even if it is not congruent with their mission.

In *Time* magazine we read of "Crime in the Suites" describing large corporations being convicted of "obstructing justice" (LTV chairman), "illegal billing" (General Electric), mail and wire fraud (E. F. Hutton), fraud (E.S.M.), missing bank funds (Jake Butcher, Tennessee banker), and failing to report large cash transfers (Bank of Boston Corporation).[3] We hear of struggles with workers' rights being described as not "union busting 101. . . . This is advanced union-busting."[4] These are examples of loss of contact with the morality and mission of the organization.

Organizations can keep their mission in focus if they can remember their history and can tell it. Such a process keeps alive the mission in the culture of the group. However, when both people and organization are out of touch with their own thoughts and feelings, they become progressively numb. As a result, they are less able to focus on anything outside themselves, even if that is the very purpose of the organization.

The next process we will discuss is perhaps best described as *distorted thinking process*. This kind of thinking process relies heavily on *externalization*, the process whereby an organization assumes it is normal for people in the organization to work out their personal issues on others in the organization. This behavior is accepted in the addictive organization; however, it wreaks havoc and contributes to confusion.

We encounter this phenomenon in organizations with key persons who are addicts. They are not dealing with their addictive diseases in treatment or in AA groups, so they externalize them in the workplace.

Externalizing issues can be seen at many levels, from the executive having trouble with his wife and taking out his feelings on his secretary to the organization itself fixing blame on other organizations for behavior that causes a slump in productivity. The purpose of externalization is to place the issues inappropriately on someone or something else, so that you, as the source, will not have to deal with it. In organizations where addictiveness is high externalizing takes places because the group is always symbolically protecting its secret and/or its "supply." These people cannot afford to see what they are doing. Externalization leads to disrespect for oneself and others. Unfortunately, it is so common that it is often accepted as standard operating procedure. Many employees say, "Well, that is just the way it goes," and resign themselves to being dumped on by others. Both the person who does the dumping and the one who receives it collude in keeping the system going; both must distort their feelings and the object of their feelings for externalization to work.

Another distorted thinking process (defense mechanism) that we see in addictive organizations is *projection*. Basically, projection is taking something that is going on inside, placing it outside, and reacting to it as if it indeed were coming from another person or organization. We see this kind of thinking in the alcoholic and in the paranoid.

When an organization is involved in projection, it is institutionalizing not taking responsibility. An organization that operates out of a distorted thinking process using projection takes all its own problems and woes and blames them on the market, the economy, and other corporations. This kind of corporation is willing to face anything but itself.

Responsibility is always linked with blame, and the organization simply will not look at itself. Hence, all its problems come from outside. The byword of the addictive organization is "if only."

The last of the distorted thinking processes of the addictive system in organizations we want to discuss is *dualism*. We have said a lot about dualism at other places in this book. We will focus briefly on some of the organizational aspects of it here. In planning, dualistic thinking is deadly, because it limits options to two or the multiple of two. These multiples are usually none other than the original positions in disguise. In the addictive organization, dualism in planning is always a form of control and competition. It prevents people from looking at their choice and the choice of others for creative solutions, which usually cannot be predicted and controlled.

Dualistic thinking sets up sides and establishes enemies. It sees other groups and individuals as the good guys or the bad guys. This simplifies relationships by removing ambiguity and subtlety. Organizations that do not think dualistically let themselves see that a competitor may have something they can learn from and in fact, they may work cooperatively in some areas. Dualistic thinking obviates this kind of knowing. It is arrogant knowing that comes out of the pressure to know everything.

We were working with a European company that had only one competitor. Our client company was sorely in need of a new organizational design. We suggested that they consider their competitor's design because it worked well. They dismissed our suggestion without a moment's hesitation because it was tantamount to admitting the other company was better. In fact, in this one area the other company could be emulated, because they did have something that worked.

ıpany's dualistic thinking was a box that prevented
... from using what was good because they felt they
would lose all identity if they borrowed an organizational
design. As it happened they devised a very complicated
design that plagues them to this day.

This example suggests the other result of dualism. It
allows one to stay stuck. By staying in the we-they mentality, our company could never take the focus off a two-sided
mentality and ask, instead, What do we as an organization
need to be effective in this product area? They needed to
look inside and begin by making themselves open to all
options.

The question they needed to ask is based on humility
and truth and is one that addictive organizations rarely ask
themselves. If they did, the answer would take them away
from the illusion of simplicity and plunge them into a world
of complexity and ambiguity.

These are only a few examples of the kind of communication and thinking patterns we find in addictive organizations. We find that management and personnel issues are
also fraught with the effects of the disease. We turn now to
a consideration of these issues.

MANAGEMENT AND PERSONNEL PROCESSES

DENIAL AND DISHONESTY

Denial is not allowing oneself to see or know what is
really going on. It is a type of dishonesty. Dishonesty is
related to lying to or misleading the self and others.

Organizationally, a company is in denial when it routinely refuses to see or acknowledge what is happening internally and/or in its markets. Companies that persist in

producing and marketing products that are harmful to the environment are in denial about their effect on consumers, and they are often dishonest in reporting to regulatory agencies. The disaster at Chernobyl is an example of a whole nation in denial. They cannot afford to let themselves know what really happened there, and they subsequently lie to the world about the disaster. Actually, even placing a large atomic reactor so close to a population center is a primary form of denial. Denial is not always on this scale. A department can be in denial about conflicts in the department. Or an organization that has been seen as on the "cutting edge" for years can deny that this is no longer accurate.

Before the popularity of such concepts as MBWA (management by walking around), executives were often removed from the "common people." Why? They were not responsible for what they did not see. We have found that it is not possible to be into "a selective denial" as an organization. Denial is a phenomenon that progressively pervades the processes of a company. You may start by denying that there is one dysfunctional manager; before long there are many processes in the organization that one refuses to see for what they are. We believe that this is because of the holographic nature of organizations and the contagion of the addictive disease.

Dishonesty arises from within the organization alongside denial, and it takes other forms as well. In organizations in which dishonesty is the norm, there is a belief that if you are honest, the organization cannot possibly survive. In such cases, dishonesty is functionally related to the resistance to change at every level of the organization. For example, if people began to say what they really feel and really want, there is a belief that it is not possible to preserve the organization as it is (this may well be true). Addictive organizations have institutionalized dishonesty.

Perfectionism is also related to dishonesty, as it is not possible to maintain an illusion of perfectionism without keeping information from others. Perfectionism requires institutionalized secrets and dishonesty.

Sometimes the demands of the system itself are so great that dishonesty is encouraged and even necessary. In this kind of situation, dishonesty maintains the status quo.

We know a cardiac department in a Northeastern teaching hospital that took six new residents every year with the understanding that only three would be kept. This kind of competitive environment put so much pressure on the residents to succeed that they did not always ask legitimate questions for fear they would be seen as dumb. They also covered up their mistakes, thus missing opportunities to learn from failure.

The system tended to put unreasonable demands on young doctors and thereby encouraged dishonesty. In this kind of system not only do the residents suffer, but even more serious, practicing their dishonesty produces a situation in which the consequences of their ignorance and lack of experience could have been severe trauma or death. We should never underestimate how far-reaching the effects of organizational dishonesty can be.

The systemic nature of dishonesty is that once dishonest communication and practices become established in an organization, they are assumed to be normal. Consequently, the only way to survive and progress through such a system is to enter into the process. It then becomes a closed system with at least two levels of communication: what is said and what is meant, or stated and unstated goals. You can appreciate how exhausting it is to operate in such a system. Organizationally, it is not likely that honesty and dishonesty can exist side by side. As dishonesty flourishes in the addictive organization, the groups and the individuals progressively lose touch with their skills for being honest and direct, and the entire system suffers.

ISOLATION

*Gary is to the Clark's
dedicated ISOLATING Enrolling function*

Addictive organizations become more isolated the more they sink into their disease. For one thing, isolation keeps other people from seeing what is happening. It allows one to persist in seeing one's reality as the only reality. Organizations become isolated when they do not include information from the outside environment in their planning. This is increasingly an issue for multinational corporations. They know they must keep cultural, human, and environmental factors in the forefront of their planning.

Sometimes dysfunctional managers use isolation as an excuse for team building. Remember the Fortune 500 vice-president who appeared to be an active alcoholic? He had sequestered himself so that an intervention about his alcoholism was impossible. In addition, he had requested to move his division to a separate building so they could "develop a more distinct identity." In fact, this supposed move toward autonomy was a foil for a manager and a unit that were severely troubled. The strategy was to get off by themselves and fix it before they went under, or at least to keep their nonfunctioning as secret as possible.

Organizations practice isolation when they stay out of touch with the consumer, those they serve, and with the society at large. Profit-making organizations are usually more adept at staying in touch with consumers because their market share depends upon it. Nonprofit organizations are frequently prevented from staying close to those who use their services by their very structure. Often decision makers in service organizations rarely have any contact with the clients they serve.

Isolation means remaining in your own reality without concern for employees or the community in which the company exists. The partners in a prestigious law firm were unapproving when an associate suggested that they do *pro bono* law work one evening a week. They felt they worked hard enough (on the paying cases) and saw no need to volunteer as well. Aside from this one associate, the others believed they had no obligation to give back anything to the community in which they practiced. Nor did they feel the needs of the poor had anything to do with them.

SELF-CENTEREDNESS

Self-centeredness is related to isolationism in organizations; when an organization feels that it is the center of the universe, it sees no need to include any other information in, for example, its planning.

We have worked with a man in Germany who comes from a long line of bankers. For generations his family has been involved in banking in Germany. Recently his bank was bought by an American bank. Immediately, things began to change. In Germany, banks are very involved with their towns, their customers, and their employees. The German banks feel they have civic responsibilities. They are often a major force in the community. The American bank only wanted to make money and abandoned all concern about responsibility to the town and customers. Our friend sadly left the field of banking because he felt that the way the bank now functioned was unethical and was raping the community. His bank had taken on the destructive characteristics of an addictive organization, and he had to leave.

Some observers would contend that this is just an example of the effects of change, and they would analyze it from a traditional organizational development framework. However, we know that self-centeredness is one of the symptoms of a much larger problem, the problem of the addictive process in organizations. If only one thing, self-centeredness or isolation, were manifesting itself in these companies, we would agree that normal changes were bringing about a maladaptive response. However, when these and other characteristics exist in a constellation, we are led to observe that a more systemic problem underlies what is seen on the surface.

JUDGMENTALISM

Judgmentalism is a characteristic of the addict. It is very different from making choices or deciding on a course of action. Judgmentalism is adding the element of "bad" to an observation or choice. There is a great deal of difference between saying, "I don't like that," or "I will not be involved in that," and saying, "You are bad," or "That is bad." Judgmentalism requires separating from and judging the other, and is nonparticipatory. In the AA program, there is a saying, "You have a disease; you are not your disease." It means you are a good person, and your disease is not you. It is separate and is something that is overcoming you.

Addictive organizations do not make this distinction. You are your actions, and you are your disease. This is the essence of judgmentalism with people and with organizations. Look at how confining judgmentalism is when applied to personnel practices. It automatically means that many standards are established for behavior and used to measure the worth of a person. Judgmentalism in corporations means that employee evaluations are dreaded because employees come out deflated or exalted, depending upon the judgment. Truth is frequently lost in judgmental corporations. When companies can separate a person's worth from his or her behavior, then information input can be utilized for growth and change. Judgmentalism in organizations actually prevents growth. It stunts growth, promotes stasis, and puts people on constant alert, lest they be judged.

Judgmentalism is extremely limiting to creativity in organizations because creativity cannot be controlled. Creativity depends on both success *and* failure. Employees who feel judged take few risks and limit their creativity. Some of the high-tech, high-performing companies have tried to alter this tendency toward judgmentalism by actually rewarding employees for submitting all kinds of creative ideas, regardless of whether they are implemented or even sounded reasonable. In this way, creativity without judgmentalism is fostered.

Judgmentalism is also related to gossip. We have noticed that in groups with little or no judgmentalism, there is no gossip, yet people talk about one another a lot. The difference is that in a judgmental system, gossip has an edge on it and is often intended to hurt and defame. It is filled with judgments of the person being discussed. When people are not judgmental, they recognize that others are persons like themselves, and they can speak the truth with unconditional love and caring for the other. Within such a paradigm there is never the intimation that the person is either bad or good, the person is just who they are. When this fact is appreciated and known in nonjudgmental groups, gossip withers.

PERFECTIONISM

Some people are surprised that perfectionism is a characteristic of the addictive organization. They wonder how such organizations can even aspire to perfectionism when every indicator is that they are in internal chaos. Still, part of the disease of these organizations is the belief that it is possible to be God, as the addictive system defines God. This is a God of the "omni's": omnipresent, omniscient, and omnipotent. The experience of the executives and company alike is to try to be God, then to fail, then to be depressed. When Peters and Waterman counsel, "Stick to the knitting," meaning do what the company knows best, don't launch out on grandiose new projects, they mean, Don't try to be God, be who you are, that is enough.

Perfection, like control, is an illusion. In order to perpetuate the illusion of perfection, one must live with constant denial, avoiding the obvious. We are not perfect, we are just people. Organizations institutionalize perfectionism in job descriptions, for example. When we are working with an organization, we often ask to go over their job descriptions. We have found that most job descriptions describe jobs that simply could not be accomplished by human beings. There are frequently far more objectives in them than any five people could accomplish, but they are given to employees as if they are real. The same is true in service organizations and human development agencies. They develop far more goals than could ever be met in the lifetime of the organization, and frequently, they are too lofty to be met. We see goals like "the alleviation of world hunger," "the elimination of racism," and "the development of all women in the Third World" in these organizations. The God-illusion and the perfectionism illusion die hard in these groups. With the pervasiveness of the addictive system, it is truly grandiose to believe that such goals will be accomplished. Addictive organizations promote the process of developing unattainable and perfectionistic goals, we believe, because it is a way to keep pressure focused on the future, to feel good about themselves from the outside and not to deal with the here and now. It is a way of maintaining an illusionary system. Unfortunately, eventually it leads to depression for individuals and organizations.

CONFUSION AND CRISIS ORIENTATION

All addictive organizations are marked by confusion. The confusion is punctuated periodically by a crisis, which serves to take the attention temporarily away from the constancy of confusion. Executives and planners make the assumption that crisis can be reduced if confusion is reduced. Unfortunately, they see the two as separate.

In the addictive organization, everyone is trying to find out what is really going on with the firm and believes that it is possible to get such information. Of course, these efforts are futile, because it is frequently an illusion that anything is really going on in the first place. There is very little real productive activity in the addictive organization, or if it takes place, it is taking an inordinate amount of effort; that is what the confusion or the crisis orientation is hiding.

Many people in addictive organizations believe that it is possible to "figure out" what is happening in their organization. This process is similar to a process called "stinkin' thinkin'" identified in AA circles. Stinkin' thinkin' is the confused thinking process of the active addict. It tends to be logical, rational, obsessive, and paranoid. It is qualitatively different from normal thinking. The belief that it is possible to figure out the confusion in the addictive organization is stinkin' thinkin' because it keeps one in the same system that is causing the confusion. To believe an addictive system is understandable is crazy. In the end, figuring out becomes a compulsive activity and never really makes a difference.

Confusion keep us in the past. We are constantly going back to understand how we got to such a mixed-up place. We consult with a number of organizations that say to us, "You have to understand the history of this." Of course, no one agrees on the history. We have learned an important lesson from conflict mediators about understanding the history of the issue. They say that one should never attempt to negotiate the past. Few people will agree on the past. They all have different memories, and everyone stays stuck on something that is over. Instead, one should negotiate present and future agreements. The same is true in addictive organizations. The confusion keeps people figuring out the past and too busy in the present trying to see what is truly going on to know about the current situation.

Crisis has a slightly different function in the addictive organization. Like confusion, crisis keeps us from being effective in our work because we leave the routine to handle the crisis, but the other function of crisis is that it is a substitute for other feelings. In the addictive organization, feelings are not permissible, and people are generally dead to what is going on inside them. A crisis creates a great upheaval and intense feelings. One of the reasons organizations create crisis is to feel. Another outcome of crisis is that it brings together people who feel alienated from each other in the day-to-day work. Crisis lets people lay aside their animosities to cooperate for the greater good. In these two ways, crisis creates a false sense of camaraderie. It is fake, it is temporary, and it is a substitute for real life and a healthy organization. It leaves people with the illusion that if they can pull together through this crisis, they really are a group. The organization absorbs this illusion and uses it to maintain itself.

The other way crisis orientation keeps the addictive system intact is through the power it gives various control mechanisms. In crisis we allow people to take over and enact unusual procedures. Crisis feeds on the illusion that control can bring the situation under control. Crises are used to excuse drastic and erratic actions on the part of managers, and they heighten an organization's tolerance for addictive behavior. Ultimately, crisis reduces an organization's ability to plan or to take responsibility. Individuals have fewer responsibilities in crisis as management gathers power to ride out the problem. When crisis is the norm, management tends to assume an unhealthy amount of power on a daily basis.

SEDUCTION

We want to discuss seduction as a model for unclear relating in the addictive organization. Seduction, which has sexual connotations, has wider implications than just the sexual. We see seduction as a process of luring people away from their own perceptions and their knowing what is right for them. When people come into a relationship with low self-esteem and feelings of inadequacy, they try to fill up from outside themselves what they lack or need. Seduction is using the other as an object and as a way of avoiding intimacy with the self and with the organization. We believe that it is a model for the kind of relating that goes on in addictive organizations.

In the addictive organization, people often find themselves getting on bandwagons or being pulled into activities that do not feel right to them. We have worked with people in a large cosmetics firm who attend meetings that are run like pep rallies to get salespeople fired up. Our client believes in the product she represents; nevertheless she is somewhat uneasy with the backslapping, hugging and kissing, hooting and hollering of sales rallies. She feels seduced and that her intelligence, and even her personhood, are being ignored or not respected.

In organizations where the norm is seduction, people feel the expectation to do things they do not want to do, or are pulled into activities with which they feel uncomfortable. The organization supports seductive behavior by having no norm by which a person can test the appropriateness of these activities. Moreover, by promoting seductiveness, people never find a way to genuinely connect with one another. Interestingly enough, seduction avoids intimacy. It uses superficial relating to avoid any real meeting. Co-dependents and ACOAs frequently have trouble with boundaries. It is hard for them to know where they end and someone else begins. As a result, they believe that normal relating means being absorbed by the other or absorbing the other, a dualism. Seductiveness flourishes in such an environment. It can be a substitute for the hard work of relating honestly, openly, and clearly to the group and to others.

Setting Up Sides

Earlier we described dualism as a thinking process of the addictive organization. One organizational process of the addictive organization is setting up sides. In this process, people think they are expected to take sides around issues. They have to be for one or the other person, idea, or product—or for the other. There is no awareness that both sides could be right, or neither, or part of one and part of the other—or that there are more than two sides. It is not recognized that options do exist.

In organizations that operate with this process, it is very seductive to take a side, because it engenders an identity and a feeling of belonging. Conversely, it feels dangerous to stay out of the process, because the social organizational norm is to join. It takes a lot of strength to avoid this game.

Co-dependents and ACOAs panic in this type of situation. In their families of origin, which were fraught with conflict, taking sides was always an expectation and a lose-lose experience. Having to do the same thing in organizations is terrifying for them; however, it is a familiar process and one that co-dependents and ACOAs may be very adept at doing.

MANIPULATING CONSUMERS

As we will see later, control is structured into the addictive organization. Control and dishonesty are combined in manipulation of the consumers, which is a common process of the addictive organization.

Organizations ask employees routinely to cover up for faulty products or faulty functioning (keep secrets). The organization participates at two levels of dishonesty here. It knowingly makes a defective product; then it markets it, asking employees to continue the lie.

Television and other media promote a host of products. Many of them are addictive in themselves (liquor, cigarettes, and coffee) or unhealthy (sugared cereals and processed foods). We have found a direct positive correlation between the amount of advertising and the unhealthiness of the product. The media creates a need in the consumer for products that are not good for them or their children. The "education of the public's taste" goes even beyond the United States to the Third World. In one of the most well-documented cases, infant formula was promoted among Third World mothers, who were encouraged to stop breast-feeding their children. This was done by representatives of the formula company dressed in white outfits resembling those doctors and nurses wear. The mothers began using the formula, but they could not afford to buy the quantities they needed to feed their children adequately. They began diluting the formula with polluted water, and the infant mortality rate soared where this formula was marketed. The infant formula case is only one of many examples of the United States exporting consumer manipulation, and consequently disease, to other countries. It is one thing to present consumers with products they want, another to convince them to buy products they do not want or need and that are harmful to them.

Using our perspective of the addictive organization, we can see that the organization forms a co-dependent relationship with the consumer. Just as the addict and co-dependent need each other to stay in the addictive system, so the company needs the consumer to remain in business. If the consumer does not naturally need the product, the company finds a way to create the need, usually through dishonest advertising or market strategies. Consumers suddenly find they have needs and wants they were unaware of before and buy the product, and the cycle continues. When either party to the relationship makes a new demand or changes the relationship, the other party has the opportunity to pull out or change also. For example, consumer rights groups have pressured companies to stop using harmful preservatives and dyes in foods. Corporations have complied, but usually because they want to preserve the relationship with the consumer and thereby keep the consumer's money coming in.

All the above processes are organizational dimensions of an addictive system. Individual addicts and co-dependents operate with these characteristics in their personal and professional lives all the time. The organization itself takes on a "persona" that is the composite of the individuals, and it is also more than just the sum of the individual parts. Many of the characteristics we describe have existed in companies for years. They are bigger than the individual personnel and more far-reaching. Many have also been considered normal operating procedure. This is one reason they are so insidious and difficult to detect and change. We want to emphasize here that these procedures are not normal. They are normal for an organization that has become an addict, and there are alternatives.

STRUCTURAL COMPONENTS

We want to consider one more aspect of the organization as addict by looking at the way the very structure of the organization is set up to perpetuate addictive functioning. We have asked ourselves the same questions about organizational structures that we ask about the addict. What do we know about organizational structures that is like the addict? We know that many structures are set up to engender competition, heighten control, apply punishment, guarantee predictability, and make accomplishment of the mission of the group extremely difficult.

We know from observing many organizations that as the system gets sicker there is a proliferation of structures and rules. As the individuals inside the addictive system become sicker, they cannot be trusted to use good judgment. In an attempt to control for this, an abundance rules and procedures are set up. This may be what traditional bureaucracies mean by red tape. It is the belief that since humans are so unpredictable and unreliable, systems can and must be perfected that protect us from the error of these humans. Of course, developing rules because of untrustworthiness is an addictive process in itself.

The structures and procedures we want to examine are all, to some extent, involved in the myth that rules will alleviate the disease of the addictive system. The most glaring system problem we find in the addictive organization is that the structure of the organization is not established to be congruent with the mission of the organization. In fact, in many cases, the structures actually interfere with, are counterproductive to, accomplishing the mission or completely eliminate the possibility of accomplishing the purpose.

One example we encountered is in a highly innovative continuing education institute for adults. The mission of the institute is to foster adult learners, who take the initiative to develop their own learning, select appropriate learning activities, and determine what they need to know to be proficient in their chosen field. Because all candidates are already professional people, it can be assumed that the institution will treat them like adults and help them meet their goals. Right? Wrong.

Instead, the institute is set up in such a way that students have to engage in activities irrelevant to their chosen field, produce reams of paper to impress administrators, and meet senseless requirements. Everything in the system militates against the candidates' becoming self-directed people. Their major process learning is to become rule followers. Many do accomplish their educational goals, but always with an eye turned to the institute's administrative structure. Much of their attention is given to playing the game just enough so that the institute is kept off their back and they can do their work. Of course, they find ways to get around the rules (usually through some form of dishonesty). Again, we all recognize this example, shake our heads, and say, "That's just the way it is." That is the way it is in an addictive organization. There are alternatives.

Here, then, is the perfect paradigm of the organization as addict. Candidates are attracted to the institute because they believe in the institute's mission and stated purpose. The administrative structure is such that the mission cannot be achieved. The structure is based on a need to control; in fact, the structure actually interferes with accomplishing the goals of the organization. The candidates, who are now confused and angry, try to pursue their goals through avoidance of the structure and dishonesty with the administration. They by necessity become cons. Administrators feel they cannot trust students, so they create more rules to ensure uniformity and high standards. To complicate matters, it is an innovative institute and afraid of "what people might think" if they appear too lax, so rules proliferate. They then get into impression management, which is a form of dishonesty. Now they are beginning to look just like every other traditional school. The mission and the structure are not congruent, and they are in trouble organizationally.

Organizations begin to have difficulty whenever they move away from processes that are congruent with their unique mission and try to be something else. Their problems then show up in their structure, because the structure reflects and implements the real identity of the company.

External referencing is a process of the addictive organization, and it is applicable here. A group is referencing externally when the only real source of validation is outside itself. It looks externally to get clues on how to behave without balancing this information with information from inside to see what is right. Co-dependents and ACOAs spend their lives looking outside themselves for direction about how to act and react.

Let us look at the profession of clinical psychology as a good example of this process. Clinical psychology, which presumably has a mission to heal the psychological ills of clients, historically has felt it is a lesser child of medicine. In order to gain acceptance from medicine, it emulates the medical model. Over the years, one can see psychology becoming obsessed with developing regulatory structures, becoming more rigid and more rule-oriented as a profession. This has resulted in a general acknowledgement that psychology is becoming grossly out of touch with the real needs of clients and is self-serving in many of its processes.

When organizations set up structures that are not congruent with their mission and look outside themselves for clues about how to act structurally a kind of organizational schizophrenia can develop. The inevitable result is internal chaos, along with repeated attempts to get control of what is happening. In fact, control is the next system problem we will consider.

Dishonesty and denial may be the clearest characteristics of the individual addict, but *control* is the prime characteristic of the addictive organization. Perhaps because organizations are so complex, they look to control as a method of reducing chaos.

Structurally, control is built into every level of the addictive organization. In an addictive organization, personnel practices are built on concepts of punishment. In this type of system, there is a belief that behavior reflects a person's goodness or badness. It is not a system in which logical, clear consequences of one's behavior are built in as a result of choices made.

The addictive organization wants to control how it is seen by others—and believes it can. This image (actually an attempt at impression management) supposedly is created by dress codes, appearance at certain functions, the discussion of some topics and not others, and a host of other actions all developed to give the right impression.

The right impression is part of the desire to appear all right to other organizations, clients, and the public. It is believed that if the outside world saw the company for what it really is, they would not do business with it or they would find the flaws in the system. This is reminiscent of the addictive family that is falling apart inside but appears to be ideal in every way to the surrounding neighborhood. Maintaining these illusions takes a great deal of energy.

Planning can be a form of control in the addictive organization. Addictive organizations truly believe that planning is a way to ensure that the future will go a specific way. They engage in long-range planning, feeling secure that the plans themselves will give them control of what is happening. For them, planning is prediction, and prediction is control. Healthy organizations do plan, but the difference is that their planning is a process, assumes flexibility, and is not used to fix unaddressed ills. Planning in a healthy organization is not an outcome. It is a description; it is not a prediction or a prescription.

In addictive organizations, planning is an illusionary activity, because the planning process actively limits the amount of information the system will take in. Addictive organizations do not sample widely from inside and outside the organization. They are very careful about who they listen to and where they go for information. As a consequence, future plans at some level perpetuate the present system, thus giving the impression that change is happening. To enhance this impression, they may perhaps make a few inconsequential cosmetic alterations.

Though planning is illusionary in an addictive organization because sufficient information is not solicited, power, on the other hand, is controlled by giving only partial information. When only partial information is given, people always feel a sense of uncertainty and dependence on others; they never have all the information they need to make informed decisions. Such lack of information leads to hypersensitivity among individuals and infighting among groups. We rarely see cooperative problem solving in an addictive organization. The form of control we see in addictive organizations puts the power in the hands of a few manipulators, and coping with it wastes energy that could otherwise be spent making the organization more effective. Schaef has observed that in the addictive system people would rather be in control than risk getting what they want and need. She means that people who risk knowing and asking for what they want, without manipulating others to get it, at least have the possibility of getting what they desire. But those who focus on controlling others get to experience control and frequently do not have the option of getting what they want. This often happens in addictive organizations where power is in the hands of a few and control is the main mode of functioning.

In addictive organizations, power and control are also exerted through structures that replicate our present political process. Power in these systems is the ability to get someone else to do what you want them to do. Inside organizations, coalitions and power groups are formed that use the political process, hence promises are often made and rarely kept. People are approached as objects and a means to an end, although superficially they are treated with the utmost respect and friendliness.

The political process is, in fact, a model for organizational functioning in many groups. Consequently, concepts of pluralism and democracy exist and are verbalized, but the reality is one of dishonesty, control, and co-dependence. As organizations get sicker, the addictive processes increase, and individuals and groups will go to extreme lengths to get their way.

The political process is one of the backup positions that we mentioned earlier. When new approaches do not work, or they entail risk, people go back to what they know best. The political process is deeply ingrained in our society. In a more open system, people say what they want and need, hear others' needs, and then negotiate solutions acceptable to all. However, addictive systems revert to power plays, collusion, lobbying, and manipulation as forms of control.

Another way the addictive organization practices control is through competition. Much could be written about competition as a characteristic of the entire social system that undergirds our economic system and thereby supports the addictive organization. That is not the scope of this book. We want to observe a few things about competition that are counterproductive and that indicate the addictive process in organizations.

Competition is often based on making comparisons. Comparisons are the process of making a judgment based on an external referent. Take the example of two people who apply for the same job. In the addictive system, the two applicants are competing against one another for the job, and the interviewer compares them to each other. The process is filled with judgmentalism. In a nonaddictive way of functioning, the issue is not comparing the two applicants. The issue is which applicant best fits the job, if either.

Competition is integrated into the addictive organization. When the organization chooses to set employees against each other for a reward, it is promoting a process by which people receive their validation from outside themselves. It is setting the other up as an object, and rewards come from beating out other persons or groups.

Competition is intrinsic to an addictive organization, both internally and externally. Some people have stated that external competition is necessary, claiming that they have no way of avoiding competitive relationships with other manufacturers making the same product. Our response is that there is a qualitative difference between being in business to beat out a competitor and being in business to make a product or render a service that is the best one can do. The difference is in the focus. When the focus is on advertised honesty that is backed up by the guarantee of the organization, competition is irrelevant. Is this not exactly the problem U.S. car manufacturers faced during the oil crisis? They were not ready with a high-quality product that met the needs of the American consumer. Japanese and European manufacturers did not have to beat out the U.S. auto companies; they merely learned everything they could about the needs of the consumer and delivered a good product. Competition is deep within the organization. It is a dearly held value. Yet everything in the culture and the economics of nations like Japan that are willing to cooperate with rival economies and learn from them is demonstrating that the competition paradigm may have seen its day. It is not good for employees, consumers, or business.

The last structural preoccupation of the addictive organization that deserves attention is the "form as a fix" syndrome. This preoccupation affects many organizations and groups. A "fix" is something that takes us out of touch with what we know and feel. Alcoholic families often look good on the outside, and in fact, the disease may be so hidden that even the children do not realize there is a problem. The form of the family is functioning as a fix. It inhibits knowing.

Addictive organizations believe if they can get the form right, they do not have to deal with the underlying disease process. There is a firm conviction that when structures can be perfected, the people inside them are then adequately controlled. Consequently, addictive organizations spend lots of time and attention working on structure. In this way, organizations are co-dependent with their own employees just as the co-dependent spouse is with the addict. As individuals and the corporation act more addictively, companies try to protect themselves from the effects of the behavior. Rather than deal with the disease process, they look for procedure or form to solve the problem.

We recently became aware of another dimension of the form as fix in a hospital setting. A friend of our family, in her early 40's who is a recovering alcoholic and drug addict, recently became aware of her bulimia. Her bulimia had gone untreated and was becoming progressively worse. Eventually, she entered an in-patient program for eating disorders. In the course of her treatment the staff taught patients that one of the problems they had in common was their inability to feel and express their feelings. Consequently, they were encouraged to feel and express what they were feeling. With this encouragement, our friend did indeed begin to feel. She felt her depression. Almost as soon as she began feeling depressed, the staff suggested that she take medication. This was confusing to her because she was prepared to feel the depression, learn from it, and work it through. Moreover, because she was a recovering drug addict, the introduction of potentially habit-forming antidepressants was dangerous to her recovery. Although she shared all these concerns with the staff, they insisted she would "feel better" on medication. Our friend subsequently took the medication, but the story did not end there. The medication became even more of an issue, for the staff watched her carefully; if they found her crying, they would increase the dosage. We believe this is an organization thoroughly immersed in its own addictive process. There is an obvious mixed message, "Feel your feelings, but don't feel your feelings," and this sets up confusion for patients.

The staff of the treatment center became invested in their definition of improvement and believed that a person is not well unless he or she leaves the treatment looking "perfect" in the way the center defines perfect, which in this case is not depressed. They ended up not treating her disease; they ended up asking her to fit into their form.

The medicating of our friend and the masking of her depression was not solely focused on her feeling better. It also served to alleviate the anxiety of the staff and fed their illusion that they were doing something and "in control of" her illness.

We think it is easy to see here that the issue became the staff medicating this woman so *they* felt better and more in control. Our friend's position is that they have not helped her deal with her depression. She feels that the purpose of the medication is to make the staff feel better, not to help her deal with her underlying issues.

We observed that the basic need of the staff was to feel that they had done something with this patient. But here the patient was not progressing according to their schedule.

They were requiring this woman to fit into their schedule; they had a set form in their minds about the progress the disease must take and they fit patients into that form regardless of their unique needs.

The form is a fix because it is used to give the staff validity, and they would rather feel secure in the fix than deal on a case-by-case basis with the uniqueness of every patient. The fix also takes one away from the process. Having a form to fall back on is a convenient excuse for not doing important work or not being in the present. Spending employee time and company money getting the form right can take forever; it can also leave the group with the illusion that they are doing something that will improve the service of the company.

Another example of form as a fix is the present insurance company requirement for medical and psychological reimbursement. In consulting with health care organizations, we have discovered that insurance companies have set up categories of treatable diseases along with rigid definitions about the amount of time required for treatment. Insurance companies define both the disease and the time allowed for treatment.

This type of system sets up a kind of de facto dishonesty. Doctors and psychotherapists cannot guarantee that adequate treatment can be given within the specified time limits. By accepting that they should be able to do this, they have to ignore individual patient differences. They rely on the form of the fix attempting to manipulate patients to fit the form and thus alleviate their own stress of trying to reconcile patient needs and the regulations of insurance providers. This is also a good example of the ability of an entire industry, insurance, to pass on its addictive process to other organizations. Doctors, hospitals, and insurance providers end up in a co-dependent relationship. This addictive process could not prevail if they did not cooperate with one another.

All three of the factors we have discussed—structure not supporting mission, control, and form as a fix—are built into the very structure of the organization. They are essential to the organization's acting like an addict. These are only a few examples of the structure supporting the addictive system. Control is a process by which the organization tries to be God. Structure not supporting mission is a way of avoiding doing the essential business of the company; it is a travesty. Form as a fix is a constant pursuit of something that will take the complexity out of the organization and make it perfectly predictable.

All of these structural components result in ethical deterioration, the ultimate breakdown of the addictive organization. When organizations have lost touch with their essential purpose, their consumers, and their own employees because they are into the processes and structures we have described here, they are, by definition, morally bankrupt. They are no longer able to honor the contract they have made with the society, with their workers, and with themselves. Organizations are public entities; they have an obligation to be who they say they are and to operate honestly.

Concurrent with examining the inner processes of the organization, examination must also be made of the products and services themselves. Companies that are producing materials destructive to the universe and to people are clearly unethical. Organizations that manufacture beneficial products yet encourage workaholism among employees are not exempt from criticism, for addictive processes inside companies do have social ramifications. As Schaef has stated, the purpose of any addiction is to produce a numb person, a zombie. A numb person is best adjusted to life in this society that asks us to do its work but never to say no to its destructive processes.

Organizations can be involved in the addictive system in many ways. To the extent that they are addicts, we are all affected and the society is affected. Ultimately, organizations that are addicts have a serious obligation to become healthy, for they have wide networks that spread the disease. Through it all, we should remember that they are not bad organizations getting good, they are sick trying to get well. They are hurting at many levels and are in need of recovery. We must also recognize that partial recoveries or "fixes" are not adequate. They may bring temporary relief, and they do not address the real issues.

IV

RECOVERY IN THE ADDICTIVE ORGANIZATION

Recovery in the Addictive Organization

In the movie *Hoosiers,* Gene Hackman plays a fifty-year-old basketball coach who is trying to make a personal comeback by coaching in an Indiana school with an enrollment of sixty-four students. The movie is about his efforts to revitalize a pitiful basketball team. The team goes on to win the state championship. In the process of getting to and winning the championship, several individuals' lives are transformed, and the entire town gets a burst of energy. Typical of Indiana towns, this town revolves around the basketball team: when the team is winning everyone is up; when it is losing, morale is down. The town and the team have a symbiotic relationship.

The addictive organization is something like the small-town basketball team. It affects individuals, groups, and entire communities. Its influence emanates in multiple directions. We have seen the power of the addictive process in addictive organizations. Now we need to turn to the process of recovery.

There are a few key concepts that relate to the recovery process regardless of whether it is focused on an individual or a whole organization. It is important to remember these concepts, because one's attitude toward recovery is as crucial as the recovery itself.

We need to recognize that *addictive organizations are hurting organizations.* They are in trouble internally. They are not evil and vicious groups, although they may do things that are personally and socially destructive. The addictive organization needs the same opportunity to recover as the individual addict.

It should be remembered that *addictions are progressive and fatal* in individuals and in organizations. Consequently, the recovery must be taken seriously. It is not like a fad diet that one can begin on Monday, lose a few pounds on by Friday, and go off for the weekend. There is no such thing as partial recovery from addictions. *Recovery is a process; it is not a quick fix.* It involves much more than giving up the addictive agent.

Many people have the mistaken belief that addicts who stop taking the chemical or give up the addictive agent have recovered. *Giving up the addictive agent is only the tip of the iceberg.* The disease is a process with many attendant characteristic behaviors and processes. Recovery is a process too, a lifelong process. There is a saying in AA that you are either going forward or going backward with your recovery. There is no standing still with this disease (and that is probably true of all of life). There are tools for recovery. These tools relate to every facet of one's life and need to be integrated throughout the life of either an individual or an organization.

The recovery process that we have experienced as the soundest, most effective, and most successful is based upon the Alcoholics Anonymous model and includes what is known as the twelve-step program. There are many other forms of the twelve-step program (Overeaters Anonymous, Al-Anon, Adult Children of Alcoholics, Debtors Anonymous, Sex Addicts Anonymous, etc.), and they all have in common working the twelve steps as a framework for recovery. (See Appendix for a description of the twelve steps.)

As organizational consultants, we did not come easily to our appreciation of the twelve-step program. We wondered if it was cultish or fanatical. We thought organizations might be put off by the spiritual emphasis. In short, we were a bit embarrassed by it. Surely, we hoped, there must be something in the traditional organizational idiom that would already have established wide acceptance in organizations. After searching in the organizational literature and talking with consultants with whom we worked, we found nothing better. Actually, the concept of the addictive organization is so new there is no place to search for models for recovery other than AA. Also, it is impossible to make a shift in paradigm using only concepts from the old paradigm. We had to risk new concepts, new processes, and new language.

We find that the AA model is a highly useful tool for recovery. It has twelve identifiable steps that addicts in organizations can use and apply to their situation. AA operates on a model of providing support to recovery through group meetings and individual sponsoring. It gives a firm foundation for early recovery and keeps people from isolating themselves by its participatory nature.

There is wisdom in the AA model, and one important aspect of this wisdom is a process wisdom. Many organizations, like any addict, want the quick fix *now,* especially after they break through their denial to their addictiveness. The twelve-step program is a day at a time. It teaches that people in early recovery can do just that, recover. Making major structural changes are discouraged in early recovery. AA resists perfectionism by counseling that "progress, not perfection" is the goal. It is a program that links people with others outside the organization so that isolation and tunnel vision can be avoided. And most importantly, it is a grassroots participatory movement; the "experts" are the people who are themselves recovering from the disease. This is the quality circle of the addiction field.

The AA model is simple, understandable, effective, and powerful. Like many simple things, there is much more to it than meets the eye. It is not only a program for individual and organizational recovery, it is also the basis for a radical system shift. This is what AA detractors miss about the program. They think they are listening to a bunch of drunks or sex addicts or overeaters tell their stories, when in reality they are observing the emergence of a new paradigm. How is this happening?

We have described the addictive system in the individual and the organization as a closed system, a system that is turned in on itself. As it gets sicker, it becomes more rigid and dishonest. It uses denial to avoid seeing its reality. In fact, it creates its own reality and becomes powerless over the addictive process. Because it is a whole system, partial recovery is not possible, for it is an entropic and destructive worldview that has taken over, not just a few bad habits.

We had a potent reminder about paradigm shifts during a visit to Kauai, Hawaii. Friends who have studied the old Hawaiian culture were explaining the system of Kapu. Kapu was a whole worldview. It was an approach to life that was filled with restrictions, terrors, and taboos. One form of Kapu was related to death. When a death happened, all men, women, and children were to stay inside the dwellings and make no sound. If even so much as a smoked pipe or a small light was seen or a cough was heard, the household would be put to death. Animals were not allowed out, lest they should make a noise. All talking and noises of every kind were forbidden under penalty of death. The Kapu was very strict, and people lived with the fear of it for years. The death Kapu could be declared at the death of a king or a king's child or other important persons. Because people were quite religious, they took the Kapu very seriously.

According to Hawaiian history, one day the king broke the Kapu by eating with women and allowing women to eat bananas. Through the act of one man, a whole social structure disappeared. In some ways, the Hawaiian people became a people without a paradigm. Within a year, the Christian missionaries arrived. The Hawaiian people were a very religious people, and they were a people without a paradigm. They were presented with an entirely new system of religious belief. Being a spiritual people and having been oppressed by the rigidity of Kapu, they wholeheartedly embraced the Christian beliefs. The entire process happened with lightning speed. In evolutionary time, this happened in the blink of an eye. They had been living under the fear of Kapu; the next day they were welcoming Christianity, at least on the surface. This was a major paradigm shift; it was an entire change of worldview. The stories, the legends, and the way the Hawaiians explained the world changed completely. Of course, integrating this change continues today.

The twelve-step program initiates a paradigm shift. For the addict, there can be no turning back. Total abstinence (meaning total change of systems) is required. However, abstinence is done a day at a time—sometimes, even a minute at a time. Similarly, an organization would have to be open to alter whatever needs to be changed, even its thinking and worldview. Faithfulness to the change, however, would be a process of doing it one step at a time.

Some have observed that the paradigm shift of AA requires making a leap of faith. One leaves control, dishonesty, and dualistic thinking patterns for a system of flexibility, honesty, multiple options, and perhaps, surprisingly, even greater rewards. The relationship of the organization to its consumers and its employees shifts. It goes from prediction and control, cause and effect, and manipulation to describing mutual interaction and synergistic relationships.

Lest the reader become overwhelmed by the magnitude of the changes, we should remember that as a nation we have made major changes before. Making a system shift is what happened when we went from agricultural to industrial economies and then from industrial to high-tech. The current contents and processes may be different, but the fact of this kind of change is not new.

Education about addiction, the addictive system, and addictive organizations is absolutely essential to the process of recovery. It is a prerequisite for all groups attempting to make a systems shift. Education is so crucial because addictions and addictive functions tend to be hidden and not discussed openly. Also, most people do not recognize the characteristics described as indicative of addictive functioning. Frequently, managers, employees, and consultants do recognize the characteristics and processes we have described; they just do not know that they indicate an addictive disease process. Sometimes the simple process of naming the addictive process as *an addictive process* is a relief for people, because it makes explicit patterns they have suffered from for years and have tried to correct.

We want to describe recovery and what it means in the four areas we have discussed in this book: key persons as addicts, co-dependent and ACOAs replicating their system in organizations, the organization as an addictive substance, and the organization as addict.

THE RECOVERY OF INDIVIDUAL ADDICTS

The first, a key person as addict, is in some ways the easiest recovery to describe, because so much is known about recovery of individuals.

Intervention is the most widely used process for interrupting the addictive process and getting the addict on the road to recovery by way of treatment and/or a twelve-step program. It is best done in a group, although occasionally interventions by individuals have also proved effective.

In an organization, an intervention follows these steps. First, various employees begin to identify behaviors and characteristics of the disease in the individual. Second, people closest to the addict, that is, those who work with him or her and have a chance to observe behavior, gather in a group. They share their observations with one another. It is important to have an EAP counselor or an addiction counselor in the group. These professionals can give useful information about the disease. They can educate the group about the progress and characteristics of the disease and give support to individuals who may be wavering in their willingness to confront another employee. The EAP or addictions counselor can set up the best time for a meeting with the addict and can lead the meeting as well. Third, it is important to establish a nonjudgmental attitude and environment. This is crucial throughout the entire process. By the time the group gets to the point of acknowledging that intervention is needed, the addict probably has created enormous chaos. He or she may have made many enemies and people may be resentful and have a blaming attitude. The intervention group must be helped to deal with their feelings about the person separate from, and hopefully before, the actual intervention. During the intervention they need to be able to describe the behaviors of the addict nonjudgmentally. Judgmentalism elicits defensiveness, and setting up a judgmental atmosphere may provide a way out for the addict. It is important that the intervention team knows and believes that the addict is not a bad person but a sick person needing to heal. Also, the intervention team must show that they care about the *person* and will not tolerate the *disease*. Fourth, the actual intervention is the meeting of the addict and the intervention group. Group members can be family, friends, co-workers, and managers or supervisors. The important point is that the members of the intervention are firm, clear, and caring of the addict. Intervention is not a confrontation. The person is not on trial. Each person at the intervention shares the effects of the addict's disease on him or her. This is a caring sharing in which people recognize the disease and the effect it is having on them personally and organization-ally. Group members also indicate that they want to help the addict get whatever he or she needs to get well. Those who are in supervisory positions can know ahead of the interven-tion how time off for the treatment can be arranged. It is sometimes helpful if the group has available information on treatment centers that have openings as well as places and times of various twelve-step meetings. The goal of the meet-ing is to get the person into treatment and/or into a twelve-step group immediately. Waiting until next week or a more convenient time is often a foil, and the person backs away from her/his promise as soon as the meeting ends.

Each member of the intervention group should state clearly the consequences of the addict's not beginning re-covery. The consequences are not punishment; they are the group stating unequivocally that they are not willing to enable the person to continue in the disease any longer. The consequences will be different depending on the relation-ship to the addict. For example, children in families may refuse to cover up for or ignore their parent's disease any longer. The spouse may decide it is not possible to remain married to the addict if the addict does not recover. Rep-resentatives of the company may say the consequences of continued addictive functioning are termination from the job. Whatever the consequences, they must be real, clear, and important.

It is also important that the intervention team is committed to follow up on any consequence they state. One must never speak a consequence that one is not prepared to carry out. We know a high-tech executive who did a one-man intervention in this way. He invited the addicted employee into his office. He laid two thousand dollars on the desk, and he said, "I know you are an alcoholic. You know you are an alcoholic, and everyone around here knows it. Here is two thousand dollars. If you go to treatment, your job and the money will be waiting for you when you come back. If you do not go to treatment, you can take the money and leave your job now." The employee chose treatment. Afterward the executive said of the interaction: "There was a lot riding on the intervention. We would have hated to lose him. He was very valuable to our company, yet in the state he was in, he was useless and potentially destructive to the company."

Not all interventions are successful. Sometimes persons have to lose the job and everything important before they will get help. They may have to *hit bottom* before they wake up. Companies and families need to recognize that the loss of the job or withdrawal of "covering up" may be the kindest thing ever done for the addict. In the addictive organization, there are a lot of stopgap measures. People work hard to prop up other people and the organization. This process usually only perpetuates the disease in the individual and in the organization. It may be necessary to let people fail so that they are forced to get the help they need. For those accustomed to operating as co-dependents, this sounds like drastic action. It is worth it when one considers that recovery saves the life of a person who has a fatal disease and preserves the continued use of their training and skills for the company.

From all this it is probably obvious that intervention teams need to be trained. Then, after the intervention there is continuing work. All the persons who have been affected by the addict are at some level probably functioning as co-dependents. The recovery process has only just begun when the addict goes to treatment. The family members and those closest to the addict need help to understand their part of the disease and how they are involved in the disease themselves. If the addict goes to a treatment center, the family will frequently be included in a one-week family program. Co-workers also need help, and an aware EAP counselor and consultants can work with them to deal with the effects of the disease.

We want to say something here about treatment centers. Some people have the mistaken notion that treatment centers are psychiatric hospitals or mental health centers. This is not true. Treatment centers are set up specifically to deal with addictions and addictive behavior. They often have a medical doctor on staff to monitor the physical effects of withdrawal; a psychologist may also be found on the staff. The primary caregivers, however, are the addictions counselors, who work with people on a daily basis to educate them about their disease and help them establish a solid recovery program. In the best centers, these counselors are also recovering persons. The addictive disease is a unique combination of the physical, psychological, interpersonal, and spiritual. Neither medicine nor psychology alone can provide effective treatment, and the medical-psychological model used by itself may, indeed, perpetuate the disease.

THE RECOVERY OF CO-DEPENDENTS AND ACOAS

Persons working in the chemical dependency field have found that the recovery of co-dependents and ACOAs is frequently more difficult than the recovery of the addict. It is easy to see why this is true. So many behaviors of the co-dependent and the ACOA are valued and supported by the systems in which they live and work. Unlike the active addict, who is probably obviously dysfunctional, the co-dependent may be killing him- or herself with overwork, covering up, picking up the pieces, smoothing over, or pleasing the boss. Is it any wonder that people who work with co-dependents and ACOAs say that the recovery for these people is harder, longer, and sometimes less effective than for addicts?

There are, however, steps organizations can take to work effectively with this process. *Education* is again a key element for the recovery of co-dependence. After even a few seminars for employees on the addictive process and co-dependence, participants begin to identify themselves and others. Like the intervention, the educational process needs to be nonjudgmental.

We have had fun with co-dependents by using anecdotal material illustrating typical co-dependent behavior in the office. For example, a joke going through recovery circles is, "What flashes before the eyes of the co-dependent who is about to die?" The answer is, "Someone else's life!" We have learned that learning about the disease in recovery can be fun. When addicts and co-dependents recognize themselves and laugh about themselves and the disease, they have already begun their recovery. Self-identification is the first step.

The *self-identification* needs to take place in an organizational environment in which there is safety and support. Some organizations tend to punish people for behavior that is "out of line." There would have to be explicit support from management to take the risk of identifying oneself as a co-dependent or as an ACOA. A company mind-set would have to be established that perceived recovery as good for the entire organization.

We strongly recommend that rather than relying on the efforts of a single EAP counselor, companies need to train teams of people to work with EAP counselors. There are several things such teams could do. They could prepare information, education, and support for recovery of addicts, co-dependents, and ACOAs. They could also act as a "think tank" to deal with the implications of whole system recovery in an organization. This is important, because organizations need support for recovery, just the way addicts and co-dependents do. They could train and work with the intervention team. The wider the base the company has in this area, the better it is. The company might even create the kind of atmosphere in which people who have long-time, well-established recovery programs could feel free to come forward and contribute their skills and knowledge. The company could become one that openly values health and recovery.

There is no one way an organization recovers from co-dependence. A recent case we worked with went this way: A mid-sized advertising agency with offices in several cities realized they were plagued by co-dependency. Top managers met with consultants after reading about co-dependency. They were not sure they fit the description of co-dependents, but they readily recognized in themselves the few glaring symptoms of workaholism, burnout, and a tendency to suffer at work. The managers could see that the system itself was operating addictively in relation to products, clients, and staff.

These managers made a commitment to examine corporate structure at a later time and deal with employees as a first step. Over a one-year period they spent four all-day meetings at a conference center in workshop sessions on co-dependency. The group began by learning the dynamics of co-dependency, and in later sessions they identified all the ways each person in the agency was co-dependent. These sessions became known as the "100 examples of co-dependency" seminars! The self-identification by all employees and an atmosphere of safety in the group engendered openness to learning and risking change.

In a second phase, organizational consultants were asked to observe employees at work in the agency and in staff meetings. The consultants then pointed out examples of co-dependency on the job. These interventions supported individuals in their recovery and kept awareness of the issue alive in the company.

The third phase of working with this agency will be to identify the structures and processes that are addictive in the company. We expect this phase of identification to be easier because the group itself will be clearer.

THE ORGANIZATION AS ADDICTIVE SUBSTANCE

When the organization is acting as the addictive substance in the lives of employees, it must be willing to look at itself and all its processes. A close scrutiny is unlikely without the support of top management. Intervention teams can develop descriptions of company procedures that have addictive implications. They can show how the organization models addictive patterns and identify the attitudes that feed into these patterns. But without cooperation from the whole system, change is not possible. Actually, we find that wholehearted cooperation is not always necessary, but the willingness at least to look at the data about addictiveness at all levels in the organizations is essential.

Outside consultants are most often helpful and usually necessary when the organization is examining itself as the addictive substance. This is because, if the organization itself is the addictive substance, it really does not have an adequate perspective from which to view itself. Outside consultants, one hopes, are not actively involved in the assumptions of the organization.

To be useful to addictive organizations, consultants need to develop an organizational assessment through interviews and other types of data gathering. The information must be reported back to the organization, showing the way it is functioning as an addictive agent. Outside consultants can place behaviors the organization believes are "normal" into a framework that highlights the ways it encourages addictions. Also, because the consultant is outside the organization, he or she avoids the politics attached to a change process that may challenge some of the "sacred cows" of the organization. More importantly, the consultant should not have a vested interest in certain results. He or she can model nonjudgmental descriptions of the disease and thereby help the organization take the first step of recognizing and acknowledging that it may indeed serve as an addictive substance for its employees.

Organizations that are willing to look at themselves as the addictive substance have the prospect of a long and multilevel change process. They commit themselves to examine all of their structures, especially those that engender loyalty. They may even need to examine what loyalty means in this company. The reward structure of benefits and bonuses would be important to look at. They also would need to look at the ways they promote workaholism, not just through rewards, but also in the entire culture of the company.

We worked with an international company that was thoroughly confused about work addictions. They admitted that they foster workaholism among executives. They also felt they were very judgmental about some employees who refused assignments or who worked a mere forty hours. Their culture was one that saw overwork as the norm; therefore, the people who took care of themselves and put in regular hours were seen as lazy. In reality, the group was a severely work-addicted system in which the majority of the executives were participating in a disease. Attitudes like these are what must change through openness to learning about organizations as the addictive substance.

THE ORGANIZATION AS ADDICT

An organization that is ready to face the prospect that it is operating like an active addict is probably facing the broadest and deepest changes of all. Organizations that are addicts are composed of many individuals who are active addicts, co-dependents, and ACOAs, and the systems themselves are dysfunctional. These organizations must be willing to examine philosophy, mission, goals, structure, internal systems, and the very products they make. They need to be open to seeing that the organization itself is a contaminating force in its own life and in the lives of the individuals in it and in its community.

For some groups, an unflinching examination of the whole organization may seem drastic. The willingness to undergo a thorough self-study does not necessarily mean the organization ceases to function or that changes take place all at once. Even total system shifts can proceed at a pace respectful of the needs of the group. Sometimes one or two small changes have amazing results that ripple throughout the company. Let us recall the cardiac department in the teaching hospital that took six residents and kept only three. The director of the department realized that he had a system that was acting addictively, even though the commitment of the doctors was presumably to the promoting of health. Obviously this system was not congruent with the hospital's stated mission. The people in it were dishonest and conning themselves and patients. Overall, the system was in disarray, and people were unhappy.

The department director proposed two small changes at a meeting of all the medical staff. He suggested that they agree to take six cardiac residents and keep them. Secondly, he asked them to agree to have fun. He requested that they do the two things for only one year. When the year was up, they would evaluate and decide what was indicated. His suggestions were met with peals of laughter heard all the way down the hall of the hospital. The staff had some concern about the first proposal. They feared the cardiac residents might slack off without competition; the second suggestion seemed ridiculous. They finally agreed to try the two ideas as an experiment.

At the end of the experimental year, everyone admitted that enormous changes had taken place personally and institutionally. The cardiac residents were no longer fearful of losing their jobs, so they began asking more questions, exposing their mistakes, and cooperating with one another. Everyone agreed the quality of work of the residents was significantly better than the previous year.

The second proposal was the "sleeper." Most people thought that "having fun" would mean an increase in parties, socials, and team sports. It did mean that—and more. It soon became apparent that one could not have fun if one were physically exhausted. They had assumed that fatigue was part of a doctor's life. To accomplish the second goal, the surgery schedule was changed so that no doctor operated more than eight hours a day. Herein lay the radical change. By altering the surgery schedule and adding exercise and nutrition programs for the staff, the doctor's began to experience their professional lives as congruent with their mission as healers. For some of them, this change also facilitated their confronting their own workaholism.

By the end of the experimental year, the staff was enthusiastically behind the "program," as it came to be called. They were turning out well-trained doctors, and, more importantly, their view of medicine and health had become more holistic and integrated. There was increased interest in wellness and a growing awareness of the connection between healthy individuals and healthy organizations. There were still individuals who were functioning addictively, but the overall organization appeared to have begun its recovery. There were fewer organizational systems or processes that would support the individual addict. The next step was to develop a good intervention team to deal with the active addicts, co-dependents, and ACOAs.

The point of this example is that we can think holographically about recovery when the organization is an addict. Instead of becoming overwhelmed at the prospect of whole system recovery, groups can implement a few small changes that radiate throughout the system.

When the organization is the addict both the structures and the individuals have to be involved *simultaneously*. The genius of the cardiology department was that it focused on two systems that had an enormous effect on individuals as well. The starting point can be either the individual or the system or both. However, the company must know that individuals and systems are interconnected.

The cardiology department is also an example of making a good start. However, recovery in an addictive organization entails more than a good start. A good start can be a fix in itself. Over a period of time the group will probably fall back into its former behavior if the recovery process is not continued. This is typical of the seminars and workshops employees attend. We call them "fire starters" because people get all fired up, learn some new skills, attempt them for a few weeks, and fairly quickly go back to their former ways.

Addictive organizations need to learn ways to continue recovery. The quick fix gives temporary relief; it does not bring long-term recovery. In addictive organizations new issues emerge as old ones are resolved. When the organization operates as an addict, there are always different levels of learning available to all involved. Consequently, recovery becomes a mind-set in the organization, it represents a change, and it is built in as an ongoing process.

The cardiology department made an important beginning. This change solved a few problems and developed a more holistic attitude toward medicine. They have some other layers to uncover, like the co-dependent relationship between doctors and nurses, and doctors and patients. They have personnel procedures that elicit dishonesty, overtime policies that promote workaholism, and other structures that militate against the small changes they have made.

We were heartened by the progress of the cardiology department, and we learned by studying it carefully that basic structures do need to be changed so that even small changes can radiate throughout the system. With the addictive organization, the challenge for executives, managers, and internal and external consultants is knowing where to start and then understanding that the process is ongoing.

In the previous three categories of addictiveness in organizations, the point of entry was usually evident. When the organization is the addict, one has to be prepared and willing to involve the entire organization, and one needs to be experienced to discern the point of entry. We have operated in this fashion as consultants, and we have found it extremely challenging and effective. In the case of the family-run business whose board of directors was also the family, whole system recovery was indicated. Traditionally, consultants work with one or two aspects of the system; here we addressed the entire system. We worked with the board because the dysfunctional family system was replicating itself in the board. We worked with the staff because they were protecting a number of active addicts. We were able to develop a relationship with the director that helped him to ask us to give him feedback whenever he acted as a co-dependent. This came as a shock to the staff, because no one had ever confronted the director. Modeling a nonjudgmental confrontation showed people it was possible and helped the director to show he was open to learning about his behavior and expected this in his staff. We then began working with the clients of the organization, for they were being affected by the staff and the organizational procedures. We kept peeling off layer by layer, arrived at the budget, mission, goals, organizational structure, and external regulatory agencies—we even looked at advertising and promotional materials.

Anyone who works with addictive organizations has to

be prepared to do a very different type of organizational assessment in order to bring to light the addictive patterns in the system. Traditionally, consultants get information from surveys, questionnaires, and interviews. We find that in the addictive organization, individual interviews are essential. They are anonymous but not confidential, so that the consultant can use them as feedback to the system. All the information gleaned from interviews is presented to all staff at a general meeting. The consultant presents it in a form that people can understand, sometimes using their own words from the interviews. The organizational assessment interviews are actually the consultant's intervention, much like the intervention a group does with an active addict. It is the consultant's way of nonjudgmentally showing the group their addictive behaviors, attitudes, and structures.

This analysis is different from other forms of consulting, which tend to focus on either the structures or the personnel: it brings together both. We have seen that focusing on only the structure, for example, leaves out the effects of the persons on one another and the structures. Focusing only on the persons leaves out the effects of the structure on people. Both must and do interact; however, their very interaction is usually destructive in an addictive organization.

The organizational assessment or intervention functions as a kind of *"naming."* It puts in front of the entire organization things they have always known and felt, have not been able to articulate, and have not seen as a constellation indicating an addictive organization. Even the naming produces a feeling of catharsis. Many people say, "It is all out there now." The consultant has said things no one has dared to say—yet all knew.

The next phase of the organizational assessment is probably the most crucial. After the initial relief of presenting all the information, the process of retrenchment usually begins. If the system is highly addictive, people will begin denying, backing off, and extolling the superiority of the old patterns. A frequent comment is, "It is better to stay with something we know than get into something we don't know." This is a crucial time and a time when the organization may relapse.

Another technique the organization may use is to ask the consultant to solve the problems. People do this by appealing to the consultant's knowledge and expertise (which is very seductive for the consultant). They see the consultant as the rescuer. They want a quick solution that will deliver them and alleviate their fears. If the consultant is seduced by these requests, he or she has become part of their addictive system and can no longer be helpful to the group. Once the consultant is enmeshed, the organization is without a role model for clarity and neutrality.

It is up to the organization to take the first step in the recovery process. The first step is to acknowledge that the data from the assessment is indeed true and that a change process must begin at all levels, organizationally and personally. If the consultant gets in the way of this process, neither the consultant nor the group ever really knows whether the organization committed itself to change or not. Later the consultant can again become more visible in the process, but in this first step, the organization must walk alone. It is an important first step, for it says they are committed and are able to make significant changes. This indicates they have the internal resources to begin recovery.

After organizations have made a commitment to confront the addictive system, there are various processes that in-house personnel and consultants can begin. It is important in whole system recovery that all personnel receive information and input early in the process. In a small business that was on the verge of bankruptcy, we did an intervention with some key individuals immediately because they were severely troubled and having disastrous effects on the company. Even as the intervention with individuals was proceeding, we met with all staff and provided input sessions so they could become familiar with the characteristics and processes of the disease. This helped them become more supportive of individuals who were going to treatment, and it reduced panic. It also introduced a new language that all personnel would need to learn in order to participate in the organizational system shift. They learned the characteristics of the addictive organization, the addict, the co-dependent, and the ACOA. They felt that the input sessions were so important that they were videotaped so that absent employees could get the information. They provided baseline data for everyone and emphasized an essential point: the organization must make an entire system shift, and nothing less would achieve what they wanted.

It is somewhat unconventional for consultants to give large amounts of information to organizations at the beginning of the change process, but with addictive organizations it is necessary. This is because addictive organizations are frequently deeply in denial and so enmeshed in the addictive process they think it is normal. They have no idea that it is an identifiable disease process. The purpose of early input is to shock them into awareness and to give concepts to their experience of dysfunctional behavior. By clearly identifying their individual behaviors and organizational processes as addictive, they have the conceptual resources to move to acknowledgment and then to recovery. Frequently these characteristics have been identified separately. They have never been linked together as indicative of an addictive organization.

FINAL NOTES ON RECOVERY

Obviously, recovery in an addictive organization is not a standard change process, and whole system recovery makes very different demands on managers, staff, EAP counselors, and internal and external consultants. We want to make some overall observations regarding the recovery process. In the addictive organization *recovery has to be a basic paradigm shift.* The essential nature of the paradigm to which the organization is shifting does not have a particular content. It is a process paradigm. For an organization, the process of recovery includes several factors.

It means that *recovery occurs over time.* Although employees and managers may have a sudden insight when their addictive system is shown for what it is, the experience of understanding, in itself, is not recovery. Organizations that begin a recovery process and become overly result-conscious will experience failure, because immediate results may not be visible. This one aspect of recovery may be a challenge to an organization's belief about what really constitutes productive change.

Recovery must occur at every level of function to be effective. Individuals are involved personally because of their roles, and the organization is involved because it is the context of addiction as well as perhaps the addictive agent. The organization does not have to confront all levels at once. It does, however, have to be aware that whole system recovery is the goal.

The recovery process has system implications for how we see what is really operating in organizations. Over time we have shared the characteristics of the addictive organization with managers and organizational consultants. Sometimes they have personally recognized the characteristics, but often they see them as isolated factors caused perhaps by poor communication, mismanagement, or changing markets.

We contend that one cannot view these elements as isolated, nor can they be treated in an isolated fashion. They are the *results of the addictive process* in the organization. We believe that one of the major problems with organizational development consultants is that they have not faced the implications of an underlying addictive process. Consequently, they have not recognized the form that it takes. They have not seen the whole syndrome, and they persist in treating symptoms as if they were the problem. Their approach does alleviate some immediate organizational issues; it does not confront the driving force behind the symptoms.

Our experience has been that recovery is possible. It is possible not only on an individual level, but also on an organizational level. Recovery is truly not possible, we believe, unless the addictive process is correctly named and change proceeds at all levels of the organization. One must simultaneously focus on the individual and the organization, and one must simultaneously focus on the process, the structures, the product, and the procedures. We believe that organizations can become the kind of healthy environments they aspire to be just as recovering individuals are living the kinds of lives they dreamed possible when they began recovery.

As we have said earlier, whenever we have answered the question, "What is your book about?" and described its contents, the response has always been, "I know exactly what you are talking about; you are describing my organization." We do believe that the information given thus far is important, true, and universal. Now let us turn to some of the implications of these ideas.

V

IMPLICATIONS AND CONCLUSIONS

1. What Are the Implications If Organizations Continue to Function Addictively?

We have been making some pretty strong and perhaps revolutionary statements about organizations and the way they function. In the *New York Times* article by Steven Prokesch that we quoted earlier, he says, "Many are adopting a new creed that puts corporate survival above all else. The result: a generation of ruthless management." He also states that "what is making Mr. Kearns [Xerox] and dozens of his peers so flexible and so willing to revamp their operations is a perception spreading through executive ranks—that corporate survival cannot be taken for granted. So, survival must now be the chief executive's overriding concern."[1]

The article continues, pointing out that corporations are in crisis and suggesting various responses and solutions to meet that crisis. We suggest that this "new breed" of CEO is facing the new corporate crisis the same way any member of an addictive system would. They are becoming ruthless, losing all morality and ethics, turning to overt dishonesty and manipulation, and focusing on short-term "fixes." Prokesch says, "But the new creed also means that America's chief executives are becoming reluctant, even scared, to stick with a money-losing product or a marginal business, no matter how strongly they believe in it." "Gone are the visionaries, the creators. . . . In the new wisdom, the chief executive no longer sees himself as enough of a seer to buck the marketplace for too long." It appears that these practices are "paying off for the moment." Yet, Prokesch quotes John C. Burton, dean of Columbia University Graduate School of Business, as being concerned that this new approach is supporting American managers' tendency to look for short-term results instead of "viewing their companies as businesses to be built and preserved." Is that not the way an addictive society views the resources of the planet and its human resources—the way the individual addict functions? We believe it is.

What does it mean, then, that corporations are not facing the fact that they are addictive organizations functioning in an addictive society? What does it mean that the responses and solutions to the crisis that emerge are exactly the kind of responses and solutions that one would expect from an active addict? What does it mean that CEOs and managers perceive that there are problems and seek solutions, just as any member of an addictive family would do, without confronting the reality of the addictive process? We believe that this perpetuates the addictive disease at the organizational level—just as it does in an addictive family. Workaholism, dishonesty, and control have never led to recovery for an individual and they never will for a corporation.

WHAT ARE THE IMPLICATIONS IF CORPORATIONS AND ORGANIZATIONS CONTINUE TO OPERATE ADDICTIVELY?

Organizations will continue to perceive problems and interpret them from an addictive perspective producing an addictive solution.

For example, in Prokesch's article on chief executive

officers, the analysis of the problems appears to be accurate and valid. We would readily agree (1) that organizations have to accept change as a constant and must become less static, (2) that corporate survival cannot be taken for granted, (3) that corporations cannot be as complacent as they have been, (4) that CEOs must function differently, (5) that hierarchy and autocratic methods are outdated, (6) that collegial rule is necessary, (7) that employee involvement is necessary, (8) that corporations must look beyond isolationist, national loyalty to the world community, and (9) that organizations have to move with "the market" and be responsive to the market.

However, we believe that the response to these concerns described in the article comes directly out of addictive thinking patterns and assumptions and will ultimately be destructive to the organization.

For example, when the response to the constancy of change (1) is to put corporate survival above all else, producing a generation of ruthless managers, we think this reflects a disease process and will be ultimately destructive. When the response to the awareness that corporate survival is not assured and needs to be considered, (2) is to take the position that "survival must now be the chief executive's overriding concern," we think of the alcoholic system, in which crisis is the norm and survival, not growth or creativity, is the focus. When the response to complacency (3) is to become a "global warrior," we see the displacement, projection, and denial characteristic of the alcoholic thinking process. When we hear that CEOs must function differently (4) and we read that vision and creativity are gone, risk taking is not possible, and social concerns are not appropriate, we see the constricted self-centeredness of the alcoholic system, combined with a loss of ethics and morality. When changes in hierarchy (5) involve collegial rule (6) and employee involvement (7) being preached for a calculated reason and are dishonest and ruthless ways of achieving desired ends, we know we are dealing with a sick system. When looking beyond national loyalties (8) is being used to scorn "loyalty to workers, products, corporate structure, businesses, factories, communities, even the nation," and when "all such allegiances are viewed as expendable under the new rules, with survival at stake, only market leadership, strong profits, and a high stock price can be allowed to matter" (9), we know that corporations are seeing the "right" concerns and positing responses that are directly out of the addictive mentality and therefore destructive—from the individual to the global level. These issues raised are all issues that challenge the existing addictive worldview, but because those positing the answers are not themselves recovering and do not envision an alternative system, they come up with addictive solutions. Moreover, because, in general, the analysis is sensible and appears true, people tend to give the solutions more validity than they deserve. Just because the analysis is correct does not mean that the solution offered is valid. Addictive solutions only create greater confusion.

We believe that unless corporations confront the element of addictiveness in their organizations, they will continue to posit sick answers to real and important issues.

As *organizations continue to function addictively, they will not solve their problems; they will exacerbate existing problems and develop more complex, destructive problems.* We see this pattern in the individual addict; we see it in the addictive family; and we see it in the addictive organization. There is a saying in AA that addicts never stand still; they are either getting better, or they are getting worse. This is also true at the corporate level. Addictive solutions can be nothing but progressively destructive.

As organizations continue to function addictively and become less moral and ethical and more ruthless, they will lose their influence in world markets. As we consult internationally, we find growing disenchantment with American corporations. This cannot, we feel, be reversed by the ruthless solutions now being spawned at the corporate level. Reality does not stop with the almighty dollar. People and organizations who are perceived internationally as immoral, dishonest, and unethical eventually lose influence.

As organizations continue to function addictively, they lose their best people. We have worked with scores of people who are casualties of addictive organizations. Inevitably, they are some of the brightest and most highly motivated men and women. They are the ones who stretch themselves, maximize learning, and devote time and energy to their company. However, many of them are leaving. They report that over time, they saw they were in companies that were addictive environments and therefore destructive. The companies implicitly asked the employees to remain blind to what they were seeing. Frequently, they recklessly drove them to keep the profit margin high.

The single-minded pursuit of profit, coupled with addictive behavior, left these employees with a sense of moral exhaustion and deterioration. For the most part, they decided they could not change the company by themselves, but they could take responsibility for their own lives. Most left the organization.

We believe this is one of the saddest implications of the addictive organization. People are a company's greatest asset. When organizations refuse to recover, they run the risk of losing their best people.

We recently spoke with a dean of a prestigious Eastern college who had just resigned his post. When we asked him why, he said there were two reasons: (1) he was told that he had to learn to be dishonest in order to survive, and (2) when he asked the president why he did not try to make the organization a healthier place for administrators, faculty, and students, he was told that it probably was possible to do that and the president really did not care. This dean is innovative and dedicated; he is well-respected and has received many honors and much recognition for his work. He has decided it would be self-destructive for him to stay in higher education.

A few days ago, we met a young executive on a plane. He seemed to be having trouble facing his yellow tablet, and we asked him why. He said that he was faced with a ridiculous task he did not want to do, that had no meaning, and was thought up by a manager who needed to preserve his ego. As we talked, I found out that he worked for a major international banking concern and had just left another such bank. He said that both organizations are insane. He had left one because there were no ethics, there was great dishonesty, and management had no vision. He had decided to give banking one more try. As we discussed some of the concepts we have presented in this book, he kept saying, "How do you know so much about my organization? You don't even work there!" We told him that we had studied and worked with organizations such as his and we knew their reality.

As we talked, he confided that he would leave within the year. He is certainly the kind of person we would want in any corporation of ours; he is probably the kind of person that corporations desperately need. Ironically, as corporations continue to function addictively, they drive out the very people who would make significant change and promote and support those who will lead the company to further addiction and eventual destruction.

When organizations continue to function addictively, they can expect to "bottom out" just like any drunk. Unfortunately, the drunk who does not recover usually takes several others with her or him. We think we can no longer ignore the implications of major corporations bottoming out. The effects are far-reaching and impressive. We need to see that this is the likely outcome for organizations that refuse to face that they are functioning addictively.

These implications sound dire, and we do believe they are valid. However, we also know that there are other possibilities. What if organizations do, indeed, confront their addictive patterns and the element of addiction within them and begin to recover? There are certainly some exciting implications that emerge from that possibility.

2. When Organizations Begin to Recover and Make a System Shift

In *Women's Reality,* Schaef says that the purpose of theory and a raised consciousness is to make us less ignorant than we might otherwise be and to prevent us from overlooking what we might usually miss. Theory should not be used to constrict our perceptions or to force other people and situations into preconceived categories. Because of the massive denial about the pervasiveness of addictions beyond the mere physical, we feel that Schaef's comment is apropos here. Whether one is immersed in an organization as an employee or comes to it from the outside as a consultant, the importance of a framework for awareness is its ability to make one less ignorant of what is happening.

Whenever people have heard us describe the addictive organization, they have become very excited. They usually recognize patterns they have experienced for years and have never been able to name. Unfortunately, they sometimes tend to rush back to the office and impose the information on the group in a quasi-revivalist fashion. Actually, our purpose in sharing the information we have thus far is not conversion. We hope this information will make one more alert and give words and concepts to secrets and confusion.

We feel there is no *one* way to change the addict or the addictive organization. There is no right answer. We do know, however, that awareness of patterns and processes is essential. Aware people are less naive and vulnerable to addictive behavior, and they begin to see a variety of ways they might be different individually and organizationally. Many options spring from this awareness.

We next discuss some of the implications we see from the information shared within this book. What we say is meant to be suggestive and representative. We know that much more will be generated as this material becomes general knowledge.

As addictive organizations begin to change and recover, we think roles in organizations could change significantly at many levels.

THE ROLE OF EMPLOYEE ASSISTANCE PERSONNEL WILL CHANGE SIGNIFICANTLY

In larger companies, the role of EAP has been to counsel troubled and alcoholic employees and do some social work–like functions. We foresee these roles changing from a focus on one-to-one counseling and moving toward a systems-oriented perspective. EAPs could be more effective on a systemic level of the addictive organization if they were trained to do interventions. As they acquire more expertise with interventions, they should be able to train other intervention teams and work with these teams. Ideally, EAP counselors should be recovering people themselves and have experiential knowledge of recovery. If this is not possible, they should at least have information on all types of addictive behavior and understand the levels of addiction we have described here.

We would hope to see EAPs fully integrated into human resource and personnel departments. They can be important additions to in-house consulting teams. Well-trained EAP counselors also could provide the addictions perspective to internal consultants who are more structure and systems oriented.

We are well aware that in larger companies, the human resource department is considered the "wimp" department. It is not the department that "drives" the company. We are deliberately suggesting here that for the company to move away from the addictive system, human resource issues have to move into a prominent place within the organization. The paradigm shift we are describing must occur in individuals, or it does not occur at all. At some level, the whole organization needs to become a human resource department to itself.

THE ROLE OF EMPLOYEES WILL CHANGE

Employees are the richest potential source of support for recovery for the addictive organization. The recovery process depends on individual and systemic effort. The first type of recovery for employees is gaining respect for their own process and respect for other people's process. Co-dependency flourishes when employees are boundaryless, do not know how to meet their own needs, and thereby become intrusive in others' lives.

We have observed that as employees recover, they progressively develop a keener ability to respect other people and become less judgmental. Individual recovery is always accompanied by increasing open-mindedness, flexibility, and creativity. Recovering persons have their inner resources more available to them and those around them. It is easy to see that if one is not constantly preoccupied with the disease of addiction, one has more energy and attention to focus upon work. Of course, this can have a major impact on co-workers *and* the organization.

Employees are also key to helping develop an organizational atmosphere in which openness about addiction and recovery become the norm. Employees can foster an open attitude by sharing their experiences of recovery. They can volunteer their expertise on intervention teams. In some companies we know of recovering individuals check in with one another at break time. They ask for support from other employees who have a well-established program of sobriety.

The new reliance on employees to take responsibility for their own recovery and support other's recovery may open new avenues of job opportunity. This approach also suggests a different view of how we might define personal resources in a company. For example, employees with well-established recovery programs could be utilized as speakers and peer counselors in human resources departments. Employees used this way can become a valuable resource for a company that is making a system shift. In a recovery paradigm, employees teach an organization that clear and focused inner resources are the baseline for effective interaction in work groups and teams. As people get healthier, they unleash their personal resources and become a model for work as productive and not debilitating.

People who are recovering will always serve as a barometer for the company. Recovering people are attuned to addictive behavior, and their own recovery is dependent upon not becoming involved and in honestly pointing it out. In this way, self-correction for the organization is in personnel, not solely in the system.

THE ROLE OF CONSULTANTS WILL CHANGE CONSIDERABLY

We want to say a few things about consultants because we believe recovery implies vast changes for this particular role. Previously, we have warned of the dangers of both internal and external consultants becoming enmeshed in the addictive system with which they are consulting. Enmeshment of consultants is common because the disease is so pervasive and it is difficult to not become enmeshed in it. There is a direct correlation between seeing themselves as "helpers" and becoming enmeshed. If they see themselves as helpers or prescription givers, they are likely to operate as co-dependents. If they become co-dependent with the organization, they lose their effectiveness.

We know many consultants who verbalize to clients that they are here to facilitate the clients' process, not to tell them what to do. Unfortunately, though, their language makes this claim while their process is controlling and manipulative. Whenever consultants take on the role of problem solving in the organization, the organization becomes dependent upon them and looks to them for answers. Consultants then begin creating and identifying more problems in the organization to (1) continue the feeling of power they gain by having the organization dependent upon them, and (2) to become indispensable to the organization and therefore be assured an income.

We once followed a consultant who had worked with an organization for eighteen months. The group felt they had become overdependent upon him and as a consequence had not developed an ability to do their own planning. Ostensibly, the consultant agreed with their assessment and prepared to terminate; however, in a final meeting he did a future projection with the group. The issues he predicted were all problems that could not be solved without him. The group panicked and almost asked him to stay. Fortunately, a courageous manager insisted they follow through with their decision to terminate. They eventually hired another consultant, but this time with a clear mandate to facilitate *their* process of problem solving.

Consultants to addictive organizations must face their own issues of co-dependence, enmeshment, and the need to be indispensable. When working with a highly addictive organization, consultants should have a well-established personal program of recovery. Consultants should know enough about recovery, the twelve-step program, and alternative systems that they can be involved in intervention, training intervention teams, and following up on interventions.

A consultant who agrees to work with an addictive organization should make a contract with the organization that includes the consultant's obligation to continue doing his or her own inner work. It is not possible for a consultant who is not being rigorously honest about personal recovery issues to avoid becoming enmeshed in the sickness of a group. Consultants who do not take responsibility for their own recovery inevitably project their confusion and needs upon the group.

We believe that one way consultants can avoid doing their own inner work is by hiding behind the myth of objectivity. Consultants claim to be objective. Organizations want to believe that objectivity is possible and their effectiveness is based upon their ability to be objective. Our perspective on the addictive organization and our own experience have led us to question this almost religiously held belief in objectivity. We question this concept because it involves at its core the belief that one can be removed from the self, from one's feelings, and from the other. At root, this belief is a form of nonparticipatory consciousness. To remain "objective" one becomes an object to oneself and must view others in the same way. Somehow, the mistaken idea has evolved that if one has feelings one can no longer be helpful to the organization. We have come to see that many consultants, when operating out of a dualism, either remain completely aloof or do indeed lose themselves if they allow themselves to feel anything about their clients. Either of these approaches is, of course, characteristic of the disease we have been describing.

However, the experience of the person in recovery is that it is possible to be involved and not enmeshed. Objectivity is a form of illusion and requires removal from self-awareness. Consultants can learn new ways of being participatory and involved without losing themselves; it is possible to have feelings and awareness and yet remain neutral. Often the most potent contribution a consultant can offer is his or her own reaction/reality, shared with the organization. It is exciting to be a "namer" of issues in an organization without being drawn into being a "fixer."

At a training event for executives in mid-life career change, a consultant shared an experience about his trying to write a book. After spending days on the introductory chapter, he gave it to two colleagues. They were less than enthusiastic. It simply did not sound like a very interesting book. They cared about the person and were honest in their appraisal.

During the training event, the consultant told about the input from the two colleagues as well as the range of feelings he had when getting the feedback. In evaluations of the training event, everybody agreed that the most valuable lesson there had been watching the consultant handle the feedback on his book and being able to be a part of that process. Of course, it would not have been appropriate for the consultant to use his dilemma only for his own ego, or for resolution of his personal problem; however, as it turned out, the very personalness of it added to its effectiveness and meaning for the whole group. It also modeled a new way of being open, honest, present, and vulnerable.

Relinquishing the myth of objectivity and being a *neutral participant* in our own experience and with the organization have far-reaching implications for consultants. We anticipate that the profession of consulting and the training for it will alter dramatically as some of these ideas are integrated into the fabric of its theory and practice. To work effectively with addictive organizations consultants will have to become more courageous.

ORGANIZATIONS WILL CHANGE

We do not intend to give a blueprint for how organizations will look as they leave the addictive system; however, there are several implications for organizations as they take our information seriously.

The mission of the organization would be supported by the structure. There would be congruence between the formal, stated goals of the company and the informal goals. Employees would not find themselves in activities that undermine the real purpose of the organization or spend their time on meaningless activities that support an addictive organization and do not rock the boat.

There would be awareness that the structure and the system, that is, the way of organizing the work, are integral to the company's mission and must support and facilitate the work of the organization. Organizations that produce products to enhance the quality of life would also be aware of and supportive of the quality of life within the inner organization. Organizations established to heal others would be aware of their responsibility to promote health among employees. Groups whose mission is spirituality and religion would tend to their own spiritual life as a prerequisite for promoting religion among others. Organizations whose products are distributed internationally would be dedicated to understanding diversity; they would learn to respect other cultures as vast as the globe and as deep as the individual psyche.

Organizations would be moral. The products and services would not be destructive to the universe, debilitating to the users, or exploitative of the employees. Likewise the policies and procedures of the organization would not compromise the ethics of any employee. There would be no organizational context for dishonesty at any level of operations.

Organizations would develop permeable boundaries. Boundaries are permeable only if the company can know who it is and still be responsive to information from the outside. Organizations with permeable boundaries do not pretend or protect themselves from data that challenges their most fervently held beliefs. They are constantly in the learning posture in the environment. At the same time, their sense of identity and mission is firm enough that they are not engulfed by new information. They are open to everything, utilizing what they need and letting irrelevant data dissipate.

Communication in recovering organizations would be characterized as multidirectional. It would flow among all levels within the organization and to those outside the organization. People would be, first of all, encouraged to communicate with themselves by listening carefully to their feelings and becoming clear about what they know. Out of this inner clarity, communication with others would flow. Communication would be a bridge to understanding, and it would be used between employees and others to enhance and deepen knowledge. It would not be manipulative and intimidating.

The content of communication would be important and relevant, and the purpose of communicating such content would be to enhance the power and effectiveness of all parties. This is in contrast to the trend in the addictive organization, where much communication goes on but never about important issues. In addictive organizations, communication is used to establish and maintain power bases in the service of the ego.

Leadership in organizations would be diffused and situational. Although managerial roles would still exist, the concept that every person has a leadership role and responsibility (the ability and necessity to respond) would be integral to the structure and process of the organization. Persons with executive and management responsibility would model effective leadership by functioning as learners, by sharing their uncertainties and mistakes, by encouraging others to search for new ideas, and by creating an environment in which it is safe for others to be themselves. Leaders' power would come from their honesty and from their willingness to live their own process and respect the process of other persons.

Organizations would alter their view of change. They would not be resistant to change. They would not try to elicit change for the sake of change. We know from experience that organizations would become more alive, and this aliveness would evolve as a source of change for them. Change would be a process in organizations; it would require flexibility, openness to information, and participation at all levels. Change would be considered normal, facilitative, and non-controllable.

Innovation and change are two issues every organization must grapple with today. We find that when people change their consciousness about addictive organizations, they begin to alter their view of change. For example, most organizations say they want to be innovative and change. We find that they mean "making changes" rather than change. The controlled element of "making changes" can often result in a "fix" for the organization. It gives the illusion that something is happening when, in reality, the change is avoiding any significant activity. As long as changes do not bring about *change,* the basic addictive operation of the organization is functioning as a "dry drunk" but not sober. For the addictive organization, change must involve a paradigm or system shift. A system shift implies the possibility of clarity and creativity. Halfway measures keep the organization in its disease.

This distinction between change and changes is a special challenge for consultants because they are often hired to facilitate organizational change. It is easy to assist a group to make some irrelevant changes, thus getting the praise and esteem of the group while avoiding presenting them with the the necessity for change as a system shift. Thus changes and change can be very different issues, and a consultant needs to be acutely aware of the implications of both for the organization. Again, pointing up and facilitating change will require courage on the part of the consultant.

This consideration of change also brings us to the issue of skill training for employees. What are the implications for doing workshops and seminars on communication, conflict, time management, long-range planning, and a myriad of other topics? In the addictive organization it is always crucial that skill training never become a substitute for the daily work of the recovery process; that is, it should never become another fix. However, employees do need skills and continued opportunity for growth. Hence, the consultant and the organization need to be sufficiently aware of the implications and the process of organizational recovery to know when training in various skills is needed and would be most effective.

When an organization is in the early stages of recovery, just beginning to heal from its addictive system, these other types of workshops are not indicated or useful. The organization must usually focus upon learning this new perspective on its addictive behavior. Later, as recovery, both individually and organizationally, is under way, other seminars can be introduced, and they must be integrated into the recovery perspective. Skill training is an adjunct to the recovery process; it should not be presented as substitute or solution to organization problems where the organization is functioning addictively.

Some organizations have successfully used communications training to establish a base for opening a discussion about addictive aspects of organizational functioning. It is in a case like this that some skill training may be useful early in recovery, or as a beginning step toward recovery. When this kind of communication training is indicated, it needs to be done by a consultant who is trained to recognize and pick up on addictive issues. In addition, we want to emphasize that when organizations are severely addictive, the addictive process affects memory and judgment: one must always question how much benefit skill training can be in a group that does not have the ability to utilize the learning. Until the pervasive fog of the addictive system is cleared, people will just be going through the motions of skill training.

Another change at the organization level might be time made available for people to attend AA meetings, to set up

Twelve-Step meetings within the organizational structure, or to work in various ways on the addictive process within the structure of the organization. This can be done on an individual and organizational level. There are many changes that an organization can make as it moves toward recovery.

IN SUMMARY

The addictive system is not reality. One of the implications of recovery from the addictive system perspective is that it invites us out of confusion. Perhaps one of the central confusions of the addictive organization is that it pretends to be real and does not recognize that it is an illusionary system; the addictive system and its processes are so embedded in society that this kind of functioning is usually confused with reality. We know that many of the processes and characteristics we describe here are known by organizations and organizational consultants. It is easy to dismiss the concern voiced in this book by saying, "That's just the way people are," "Organizations function that way," "The workplace has always had these problems"; and so on. We believe such statements are one way of avoiding looking at the illusionary addictive system as a nonreality. It is important to know that all of the isolated problems we see in organizations are part of a lingering and pervasive disease we call the addictive process. When we see them and know that they are indicators of addictions and need to be recognized as such, we also know that recovery and change are possible. The admission that the addictive system is an illusionary system that does not reflect reality is a significant step in recovery. It brings the possibility of seeing reality more clearly and participating in it more fully. Indeed, the knowledge that the addictive system is an illusion may well be the first step in making a paradigm shift.

Finally, we want to say something about what is implied by what we perceive about the very basis and assumptions on which organizations should rest. We are not the first to suggest that something other than economic considerations have to inform and motivate organizations. We share the perspective of organizational transformationists who believe that the rational models of bureaucracy are defunct and that broad ethical and spiritual values must inform and undergird organizations. We, of course, acknowledge that economics is important in organizations; however, whenever economics is the central consideration, organizations are headed for the same kind of moral deterioration that we see in the addictive system as a whole. We know it is possible to "have it all" in healthy organizations. "Having it all" must be seen as supporting the inner integrity of the organization and fostering utmost honesty with consumers and the community. Organizations that do this reap amazing rewards. Organizations can be—and need to be—based on spiritual and humanitarian values. They can be visionary in the society while meeting needs, providing jobs, making a profit, and performing the "work" of the society. They can also be visionary, facilitative of health, and provide a good living for employees.

Early in this book we describe three major currents in modern organizations—participation, innovation, and leadership. From our perspective of the addictive organization, these three issues are still central for organizations and workers alike. We now see that in a recovering organization, participation occurs on three levels simultaneously: participation (1) with the self and with one's own recovery, (2) with others, implying the need for clarity in relationships so as to avoid co-dependence, (3) with the organization in actively designing policies, structures, and systems that foster recovery.

Innovation is more than making cosmetic changes: it is making a "leap of faith" out of the existing paradigm of addiction that leads to slow but certain death to an emerging paradigm that embraces and facilitates aliveness and full functioning.

Leadership is not control. It is, first and foremost, a model of self-responsibility. Leadership in the recovering organization is holographic, as is every characteristic of a healthy organization: the developments that take place inside the individual take place in the system and vice versa. Leadership emanates from individuals to groups to systems and from systems to groups to individuals. Ultimately, the entire organization becomes a beacon to others in the industry and the society and becomes responsive to the society in which it exists.

We know that organizations can become wholesome places to work. We have seen this happen. We believe they can be integrated into the hologram of one's life in the society. We are convinced that organizations themselves have the opportunity to be active agents in the major paradigm shift that is occurring worldwide. We believe organizations can and will recover their ethical and spiritual base. In so doing, they have the possibility of becoming an inspiration to all of us who believe it is possible to regain anew our faith in organizations and in ourselves.

Appendix
The Twelve Steps of AA

1. We admitted we were powerless over alcohol, that our lives had become unmanageable.

2. Came to believe that a Power greater than ourselves could restore us to sanity.

3. Made a decision to turn our will and our lives over to the care of God *as we understood Him.*

4. Made a searching and fearless moral inventory of ourselves.

5. Admitted to God, to ourselves, and to another human being the exact nature of our wrongs.

6. Were entirely ready to have God remove all these defects of character.

7. Humbly asked Him to remove our shortcomings.

8. Made a list of all persons we had harmed, and became willing to make amends to them all.

9. Made direct amends to such people whenever possible, except when to do so would injure them or others.

10. Continued to take personal inventory and when we were wrong promptly admitted it.

11. Sought through prayer and meditation to improve our conscious contact with God *as we understood Him,* praying only for the knowledge of His will for us and the power to carry that out.

12. Having had a spiritual awakening as the result of these steps, we tried to carry these messages to alcoholics, and to practice these principles in all our affairs.

Notes

INTRODUCTION

1. M. D. Molinari, "The Productive, Integrated Organization" (Internal organizational memo, Cummins Engine Corporation, 1986), p. 1.
2. Anne Wilson Schaef, *When Society Becomes an Addict* (San Francisco: Harper & Row, 1987).

I: THE ORIGINS OF AN IDEA

1. William S. Ouchi, *Theory Z* (Reading, MA: Addison-Wesley, 1981).
2. Marshall Sashkin, "Participative Management Remains an Ethical Imperative," *Organizational Dynamics,* Spring 1986, pp. 62–75.
3. Morris Berman, *The Reenchantment of the World* (New York: Bantam, 1984).
4. Everett Rogers, *Diffusion of Innovation* (Glencoe, IL: Free Press, 1962); Gerald Zaltman et al., *Innovations in Organizations* (New York: John Wiley and Sons, 1973).
5. Rosabeth Moss Kanter, *The Change Masters* (New York: Simon & Schuster, 1983).
6. Ibid., p. 34.
7. C. S. Lewis, *Perelandra* (New York: Macmillan, 1944).
8. Thomas Peters and Robert Waterman, *In Search of Excellence* (New York: Warner Books, 1982); Thomas Peters and Nancy Austin, *A Passion for Excellence* (New York: Warner Books, 1985).
9. Peters and Austin, pp. 495–96.
10. William Bridges, *Transition: Making Sense of Life's Changes* (Reading, MA: Addison-Wesley, 1980).
11. William Bridges, "Managing Organizational Transition," *Organizational Dynamics,* Spring 1986, p. 25.
12. Alan Sheldon, "Organizational Paradigms: A Theory of Organizational Change," *Organizational Dynamics,* Winter 1980, pp. 61–79.
13. Manfred F. R. Kets deVries and Danny Miller, *The Neurotic Organization* (San Francisco: Jossey-Boss, 1984).
14. Paul Hersey and Kenneth Blanchard, *Management of Organizational Behavior: Utilizing Human Resources* (San Diego, University Associates, 1986).

15. Michael Maccoby, *The Leader* (New York: Simon & Schuster, 1981); Warren Bennis and Bert Nanus, *Leaders: The Strategies for Taking Charge* (New York: Harper & Row, 1985).

16. John D. Adams, ed., *Transforming Work* (Alexandria, VA: Miles River Press, 1984), p. vii.

17. Peter Vaill, "Process Wisdom for a New Age," in *Transforming Work*, ed. John D. Adams, p. 33.

18. Thomas Kuhn, *The Structure of Scientific Revolutions* (Chicago: University of Chicago Press, 1970).

19. Sheldon, "Organizational Paradigms," p. 65.

20. Marilyn Ferguson. *The Aquarian Conspiracy* (Los Angeles: Tarcher, 1980), p. 18.

21. Renee Weber, "The Enfolding-Unfolding Universe: A Conversation with David Bohm," in Ken Wilber, *The Holographic Paradigm* (Boulder: Shambala Press, 1982).

22. Charles Hampden-Turner, "Is There a New Paradigm? A Tale of Two Concepts" (Paper presented to Shell International managers, January 1985).

23. Ibid., p. 21.

24. Berman, *Reenchantment of the World*.

25. Marion Zimmer Bradley, *Thendara House* (New York: Daw, 1983); Ann J. Lane, ed., *The Charlotte Perkins Gilman Reader: The Yellow Wallpaper and Other Fiction* (New York: Pantheon Books, 1980); Charlotte Perkins Gilman, *Herland* (New York: Pantheon Books, 1979); Carol Hill, *The Eleven Million Mile High Dancer* (New York: Holt, Rinehart & Winston, 1985), Ursula LeGuin, *The Wizard of Earthsea* (New York: Bantam, 1974); Anne McCaffrey, *Dragonsinger* (New York: Bantam, 1977); Ursula LeGuin, *A Very Warm Mountain* (New York: Bantam, 1976).

26. Margaret Atwood, *The Edible Woman* (New York: Warner Books, 1982); Mary Gordon, *Men and Angels* (New York: Random House, 1985); Keri Hume, *The Bone People* (New Zealand: Spiral/Hodder & Stoughton, 1984); Gloria Naylor, *The Women of Brewster Place* (New York: Viking Press, 1982); Alice Walker, *The Color Purple* (New York: Harcourt Brace Jovanovich, 1982); Toni Morrison, *The Bluest Eye: A Novel* (New York: Holt, Rinehart & Winston, 1970); May Sarton, *Kinds of Love* (New York: Norton, 1970).

27. Betty Lehan Harragan, *Games Mother Never Taught You* (New York: Warner, 1977); Rosabeth Moss Kanter, *Men and Women of the Corporation* (New York: Basic Books, 1977); Nehama Jacobs and Sarah Hardesty, *Success and Betrayal: The Crisis of Women in Corporate America* (Danbury: Franklin Watts, 1986).

28. Mary Daly, *Beyond God the Father* (Boston: Beacon Press, 1973); Carol Gilligan, *In a Different Voice: Psychological Theory and Women's Development* (Cambridge, MA: Harvard University Press, 1979); Elizabeth Dod-

son-Grey, *Patriarchy as a Conceptual Trap* (Wellesley, MA: Roundtable Press, 1977); Adrienne Rich, *On Lies, Secrets, and Silences: Selected Prose—1966–78* (New York: Norton, 1979); Anne Wilson Schaef, *Women's Reality: An Emerging Female System in the White Male Society* (Minneapolis: Winston Press, 1981).

29. Jed Diamond, *Inside Out: Becoming My Own Man* (San Raphael, CA: Fifth Wave Press, 1983); Ken Druck, *The Secrets Men Keep* (Garden City, NY: Doubleday, 1979); Herb Goldberg, *The Hazards of Being Male* (New York: Signet, 1976); Herb Goldberg, *The New Male* (New York: Signet, 1979).

30. *Alcoholics Anonymous*, 3d ed. (New York: Alcoholics Anonymous World Services, Inc., 1976).

31. Vernon Johnson, *I'll Quit Tomorrow* (New York: Harper & Row, 1980).

32. Sharon Wegscheider-Cruse, *Another Chance: Hope and Health for the Alcoholic Family* (Palo Alto, CA: Science and Behavior Books, 1980); Robert Subby, "Inside the Chemically Dependent Marriage: Denial and Manipulation," in *Co-Dependence: An Emerging Issue* (Hollywood Beach, FL: Health Communications, 1984).

33. Janet Woititz, *Adult Children of Alcoholics* (Hollywood, FL: Health Communications, 1983).

34. Claudia Black, *It Will Never Happen to Me* (Denver, M.A.C. Co., 1981).

35. Charles Whitfield, "Co-Dependency: An Emerging Problem Among Professionals," in *Co-Dependency: An Emerging Issue*, p. 50.

36. Anne Wilson Schaef, *Co-Dependence: Misunderstood, Mistreated* (San Francisco: Harper & Row, 1986); *When Society Becomes an Addict*.

II: THE ADDICTIVE SYSTEM—TERMS AND CHARACTERISTICS

1. Schaef, *When Society Becomes an Addict*, p. 23.

2. Ibid., pp. 86–93.

III: THE FOUR MAJOR FORMS OF ADDICTION IN ORGANIZATIONS

CHAPTER 2—TAKING YOUR DISEASE WITH YOU INTO THE ORGANIZATION, OR THE REALITY OF REPLICATION

1. Robert N. Goldberg, "Under the Influence," *Savvy*, July 1986, pp. 51–60.

2. Ibid., p. 60.

CHAPTER 4—THE ORGANIZATION AS ADDICT

1. Chris Argyris, "Skilled Incompetence," *Harvard Business Review*, September–October 1986, p. 74.

2. Ibid., p. 76.

3. C. P. Alexander, "Crime in the Suites," *Time,* July 10, 1985 pp. 56-7.
4. "Lorenza Starts His Attack," *Newsweek,* February 2, 1987.

SECTION V: IMPLICATIONS AND CONCLUSIONS

CHAPTER 1—WHAT ARE THE IMPLICATIONS IF ORGANIZATIONS CONTINUE TO FUNCTION ADDICTIVELY?

1. Steven Prokesch, "Remaking the American CEO," *New York Times,* January 15, 1987.